THE LION OF JUDAH HATH PREVAILED

RESEARCH ASSOCIATES
SCHOOL TIMES PUBLICATIONS

H.I.M. the Emperor Haile Selassie

THE LION OF JUDAH HATH PREVAILED
Christine Sandford

Introduction
Ras Sekou Sankara Tafari

The Lion of Judah Hath Prevailed

Paperback Edition
Published November 1998 by
RESEARCH ASSOCIATES SCHOOL TIMES
PUBLICATIONS & FRONTLINE DISTRIBUTION INT'L INC.
Second Printing 2009
BY ARRANGMENT WITH ORION PUBLISHING GROUP,
LTD. LONDON, ENGLAND
COVER DESIGN AND GRAPHICS BY DENISE BOREL
© 1954 CHRISTINE SANDFORD
PREFACE COPYRIGHT © 1998 RAS SEKOU SANKARA TAFARI

Library of Congress Catalog Number 97-66335
ISBN: 0 94839 041 7

INTRODUCTION

To The Research Associates' Edition

KING HAILE SELLASSIE - THE LION OF JUDAH HATH PREVAILED

"And one of the elders saith unto I, weep not. Behold the lion of the Tribe of Judah, the Root of David hath prevailed to open the book and loose the seven seals thereof."
Revelation **5:5**

Behold! The coming of a greater one. When Tafari Makonnen was born on July 23rd 1892, to his earthly father Ras Makonnen and to his earthly mother Waizero Yeshimabeit, it was indeed a glorious, miraculous, and very significant birth.

The I-Majesty's official biographer and author, Christine Sandford states in chapter four of this magnificent book, "The rain had begun in Harrar that July day - great clouds were again massing on flat-topped Kondulu."

Tafari Makonnen was earth born. He was the tenth and only surviving child from the union of Ras Makonnen and Yeshimabeit. Twenty months later on March 14th 1894, his mother died in child birth leaving the baby Tafari in the care and custody of his father.

In this book, Haile Sellassie - The Lion of Judah, the author points out that young Tafari Makonnen grew up under the watchful eyes of his father, who was a very skillful warrior, an upright, just and highly spiritual man. Ras Makonnen was also the cousin of Emperor Menelek II, thus making him a direct descendant of the Solomonic dynasty. Although, Ras Makonnen would travel extensively to Europe and other countries as an emissary on behalf of the crown he ensured that the young Tafari obtained a well balanced education in all spheres of life...civil, religious, languages and the humanities.

When Ras Makonnen transcended this life in April 1906, the youthful Tafari, then known by the title 'Dejazmach' Tafari was sent to live at the palace in Addis Ababa by Emperor Menelek. At the Royal palace under the Emperor's supervision, he lived a life of an esquire observing the affairs of the Emperor's court. This experience prepared him for higher and more annotated roles in his later years.

After serving in various official positions, for example, Dejazmach, governorships etc..the I-Majesty had to deal with growing disgruntlement and crises brewing within the palace after the death of Emperor Menelek II; the youthful Tafari stood strong to the challenge to rule and govern Ethiopia.

With the demise of Emperor Menelek, there was a political vacuum of discontent within the hierarchy of the palace administration. It began with the Empress Taitu claiming the throne and Lij Yasu, the apparent heir chosen by the late Emperor to succeed him, attempting to mislead the people by conforming, and personally yielding Ethiopia to the clutches of Islam.

Ras Tafari became Regent and heir to Empress Zauditu, who was Menelek's daughter from a previous marriage. Ras Tafari rose quickly and steadily within the ranks of authority, ie. from Governor of various provinces, to Regent, Negus or King, then finally to his coronation as Emperor of all Ethiopia. Ras Tafari and his wife Princess Menan were crowned on the same day in a most gallant ceremony on November 2nd 1930. Many nations of the world sent representatives to witness this splenderous affair. Coincidentally, his coronation was prophesied a few years earlier by an African-Jamaican born Pan-Africanist - the honorable, saint and prophet, Marcus Mosiah Garvey who is reported to have declared in a sermon one Sunday morning:

> **"Look to Africa where a black king shall be crowned for the day of deliverance is near."**

On his coronation, Ras Tafari reclaimed his baptismal name **"Haile Sellassie I"** which translates into English to mean-**"The Power of the Holy Trinity."**

It was Emperor Haile Sellassie I, who gave Ethiopia it's first written constitution on July 16th 1931. It was also the Emperor who struggled tirelessly with Ethiopian nobles and chiefs to abolish the last remnants of the slave trade from within the Ethiopian Empire. Haile Sellassie intended to build Ethiopia into a modern state - he was preparing to move her from a backward and feudal society to a progressively informed nation state. He was building Ethiopia into a country where education and health care would be attainable to all her citizens, when the thrust of war came from Mussolini's Roman Italy.

"And I saw the beast, and the kings
of the earth, and their armies
gathered to make war against him
that sat on the horse and against his
army."   *Rev: 19:19*

After the Emperor returned to Ethiopia from exile in Bath, England, he was able to lead his country to victory by guiding his troops who were engaged in extensive guerrilla warfare with the Italian invasion forces who had occupied his country. His troops consisted mainly of fearless barefoot warrior soldiers who relentlessly fought the advancement of the Italian army, with the most primitive weaponry available to them.

Although, these barefoot warriors possessed these backward armaments, their hearts were filled with national pride and dignity in defense of their African motherland. With some assistance from the British armed forces, the Emperor and his troops were able to beat the Italians to a fast retreat from Ethiopia and her borders.

When the war was over, the father of modern day Ethiopia and Africa continued to reimplement his program of construction of roads and highways, schools, hospitals and developing Ethiopia into a modern state. His greatest passions according to the author, Mrs. Sandford were education and the youth.

In reading "The Lion of Judah Hath Prevailed" one will see that Father Haile Sellassie gave much attention to visiting and contributing his valuable time and money to the building of schools, hospitals and the Ethiopian Orthodox church, formerly the Ethiopian Coptic church.

It was while serving as Regent that Ras Tafari diligently secured Ethiopia a place in the league of Nations on September 28th 1924. During the outbreak of the Italian invasion, Haile Sellassie was able to tactically use that known International talk shop as a vehicle and platform to expose to the world the aggressive Italian dictator Mussolini's hegemonic intentions.

"I, Haile Sellassie I, Emperor of Ethiopia, am here today to claim that justice that is due to my people and the assistance promised to it eight months ago by fifty-two nations who asserted that an act of aggression had been committed in violation of international treaties. None other than the Emperor can address the appeal of the Ethiopian people to these fifty-two nations. There is perhaps no precedent for the head of a state himself speaking in the Assembly. But there is certainly no precedent for a people being the victim of such wrongs, and being threatened with abandonment to it's aggressor."
Page 80, chapter 10.

Nonetheless, the western world did not take heed of Haile Sellassie plea, because of their own pre-occupation with European colonization of Africa.

"The Lion of Judah Hath Prevailed" was written by Christine Sandford in 1955, and published by J.M. Dent and Sons in the same year. It was published to commemorate the Silver Jubilee of Emperor Haile Sellassie's coronation. Although, this book is over forty-two years old, it is a sound , and very remarkable chronology and historical document on the life and some of the major achievements of this fascinating and incredible human character. It details the early years of Haile Sellassie, as emperor of all Ethiopia.

This book outlines his birth and demonstrates some forms of similarities to Jesus the Christ. It points out the I-Majesty's kindness, his humility, and his political astuteness as an international statesman. From reading The Lion of Judah Hath Prevailed, we will learn about the power of forgiveness of one's enemies,as the Emperor was able to practice. He encouraged the Ethiopian masses to practice forgiveness of the Italians who were captured as Prisoners of War. Many Italians were allowed to remain in Ethiopia without any harm after the victory of 1942. However, the I-Majesty also taught his people that they should not forget the atrocities that the Italians, under Mussolini levied on them.

Within the confines of these pages one sees both the meticulousness and patience of the I-Majesty in his dealings with the affairs of state. Yet it shows his swiftness in enacting justice and pursuing equality, and the surmountable love he has embodied for his people.

In the text, Mrs. Sandford puts the detractors of
the Emperor to shame, when one sees Father, as the
King of all Kings, the Emperor of all Ethiopia
commanding his troops on the battlefield, though
ill-equipped with backward and antiquated armaments
due to the embargo on the sale of weapons to Ethiopia by
Europe. His inspiration on the battlefront helped to keep
morale high within the ranks of the barefoot patriotic soldiers
of Ethiopia. Mrs. Sandford pinpoints in chapter nine,
"*...and in it the Emperor himself took an active part, firing
a machine-gun for two days without sleep.*"
This underscores the activeness of the Emperor being
engaged on the frontline of the actual war.

During different stages of the war he continued
to show the entire African Diaspora and his Ethiopian
people, along with other nations of the world, the need
to succumb and prostrate to the will of the Highest One,
the Creator of the Universe, Jah Rastafari. This is
indeed and example of being both human and divine. In
chapter eleven, one can see this clearly when the
I-Majesty declares:

> **"I therefore gathered my men
> who were scattered everywhere in
> pursuit of the enemy, and I am in
> my capital today. My happiness is
> boundless. I have been granted
> the opportunity to lead my own
> soldiers, crush our common enemy
> and reach Addis Ababa. I owe
> thanks without limit to Almighty God,
> who has enabled me to be with you
> today in my Royal Palace from which
> the Fascist Government has been**

forced to flee! People of my
country Ethiopia! On this day Ethiopia
indeed stretches out her hands to
God shouting and telling out her joy
to her own sons!"

Indeed, Emperor Haile Sellassie I is the Lion of
Judah. Though the jury is still out in comparing the
quality of life during the fifty-four year period when the
I-Majesty ruled his country, Ethiopia, to life under the
military Juanta led by Colonel Haile Mariam Mengustu,
or the atrocities being carried out by the current Democratic regime. History will compare his ruling with the
atrocities being carried out by the current Democratic
regime. The present regime seems to be engaged in
amassing serious human rights violations. Amnesty
International has recently documented a list of political
opponents who have either disappeared or were
imprisoned by this current regime.

However, one cannot help but assess Haile
Sellassie I, as a great leader who gave selflessly of
himself to see the development and birth of Ethiopia as
a great nation amongst the confederacy of nations.
Emperor Haile Sellassie I is the only person in the over
three thousand years history of ancient Ethiopia to be
crowned thrice, firstly, as Regent then as Negus or King
and finally as Emperor of all Ethiopia. This demonstrates
the power of the Hola Trinity.

Therefore, **"The Lion of Judah Hath Prevailed"**
is relevant more so today, than ever, especially with the
growing interest and concern around the personality of
Emperor Haile Sellassie I. Rastafarians around the
world see and acknowledge Haile Sellassie as the

personification of the Living Creator, Jah Rastafari,
King Sellassie I Liveth. For Ethiopia shall rise again
and she shall stretch forth her hands unto Almighty
Jah Rastafari Haile Sellassie.

ALL HAIL THE POWER OF THE HOLA TRINITY!

**KING SELLASSIE I IS THE LION OF JUDAH-KING
SELLASSIE I IS.**

Ras Sekou Sankara Tafari
Almighty Jah's One Perfect Love!
July 1998.

GLOSSARY

Hola   *Holy*

I-Majesty   *His Majesty*

Contents

Illustrations

The Dynasty

THE royal line of kings of Ethiopia has its origins, as do many of those in European countries, in legend and story; but none can claim a longer descent, nor an origin so substantiated in national literature and primitive picture, than the dynasty founded by the 'Queen of Sheba and her only son Menyelek.' This story forms the principal theme of one of the earliest documents in Ethiopic literature—the Kebra Nagast—composed in the thirteenth century, and still remains the subject of a series of scenes painted on canvas to be bought to-day in the streets of Addis Ababa.

Moreover it is of supreme importance politically. In his book on Ethiopia, Archbishop David Matthew makes the cult of this dynastic theory the foundation on which the realm of Ethiopia has been built up; and in the introduction to his translation of the Kebra Nagast or 'Glory of Kings,' Sir Wallis Budge points out the awe and reverence in which this early document with its evidence of Solomonian descent is held throughout the country.

Here is the story. The Queen of Sheba—or the Queen of the South—having heard, as the Bible narrative tells us, of the wisdom and riches of King Solomon, journeyed from her kingdom—according to Ethiopian legend a city near Aksum or possibly the country of Sa'ba which forms part of the Arabian peninsula—to assure herself of the truth of all she had heard. Overcome by the splendour of his court, and the certainty that he had divine protection and inspiration, the queen, who had hitherto been a worshipper of the sun and stars, professed herself a convert to the monotheism of the Jewish king, and asked for counsel and guidance that she might return to her own country and rule it aright.

King Solomon was loath to let her go for he would have gladly made her his queen.

When the queen sent her message to Solomon saying that she was about to depart into her own country he pondered in his heart and said: 'A woman of such splendid beauty hath come to me from the ends of the earth. What do I know? Will God give me seed in her?' Then the story goes on to tell how by a ruse he achieved the union with her that he desired—yet she, preferring to be queen in her own country rather than one among many at the court of the Jewish monarch, departed bearing with her a ring which should be a sign of sonship if a man child should be born. Nine months later the queen bore a son whom she called Ibn Hakim, 'and his whole body and its members and the bearing of his shoulders resembled those of King Solomon his father.' So the child grew to be a young man of twenty-two years of age, and she sent him with a train of nobles and officers to claim sonship from Solomon, giving him in secret the ring that his father had given her. Then King Solomon recognized and received his first-born son, and much against his will sent him back again with his blessing. Thus the line of Solomonian kings was established.

The ancient history of this people from southern Arabia and the story of how, later, they crossed the Red Sea to establish themselves on the uplands of its western coast can only be a matter of surmise. Yet it seems certain that some such migration or conquest must have taken place in order to account for the Semitic characteristics and culture of the people who became leaders among the tribes of the highlands of Tigre, and for the Semitic form of its language. It

H.I.M. the Emperor at
five years old

H.I.M. the Emperor at
seven years old

H.I.M. the Emperor Haile Selassie, seven years old, with Ras Imeru
(left) and Tafari Belaw (right)

is probable that these invaders from Arabia imposed their customs and their language upon the original Hamitic stock of the northern dwellers of Ethiopia; but their emergence into the actual facts of history does not take place until the middle of the first century A.D. The kingdom of Aksum which they founded is first mentioned in an account of the Red Sea and the Indian Ocean, composed by a Greek writer of the first century A.D. By this time its port of Adulis had been founded and it was from there that the kings of Aksum exported their ivory, gathered from the Nile valley, to the Roman Empire. The account mentions a certain Soscales, 'king of all these regions'; and he must therefore be accounted the first historical king of Ethiopia known to the outside world.

This Aksumite kingdom flourished during the first ten centuries of the Christian era and we have from various sources descriptions of the court of the kings and of their conquests. During the third century one of these kings extended his boundaries north towards Suakim, south to the lakes of Rudolph and Victoria according to legend, and eastwards towards the Red Sea, and beyond, compelling the kings of southern Arabia to pay tribute to him. He might with justice be considered to have founded the Ethiopian Empire.

Yet far more important than the territorial conquests of its kings was its own submission to the new spiritual forces of Christianity. In the fourth century the two brothers Aedesius and Frumentius, both Christians from Tyre, were captured when their ship touched the west coast of the Red Sea, and were taken to the King of Aksum.

Seeing that Frumentius was 'prudent and sagacious, the king raised him to be his treasurer and secretary.'[1] So well did he acquit himself towards his royal master that, on the

[1] Rufinus, quoted by Jones and Monroe: *History of Abyssinia*, p. 26.

death of the king, Frumentius was installed as guardian for his infant son. Then the chronicler tells us that 'God stirred up his heart.' [1] He begged leave to visit the bishop —at that time Athanasius—in Alexandria, and laid before him the possibility of the conversion of the Aksumite kingdom to Christianity. So he returned as bishop himself to Ethiopia, 'and a countless number of barbarians' [2] were converted by him to the Christian faith.

Thus there emerged in the high plateau of Ethiopia, which stretched from the boundaries of Nubia to the great lakes which form the central depression of the great Rift Valley, and from the torrid Danakil and Somali plains that border the Red Sea to the humid heat of the Nile valley, a Christian kingdom which gradually absorbed and converted, either by persuasion or force, the surrounding peoples. Its ancient language Geez remains the language of the Bible and, until very recently, of the Church and its liturgies, and of most of the literature; but later Amharic became the spoken language of the court and government. For many centuries the coronation of the King of Kings—so ran the title of the ruler—took place at Aksum; but the court seems to have been perpetually on the move, the king travelling around his kingdom in great state, and displaying himself on the occasion of the great Church feasts to all his people. The extraordinary custom had grown up early in Ethiopian history of secluding all possible rivals to the throne—the princes in the direct line of descent—on an impregnable 'amba' or mountain fastness, where they lived out their lives under guard, though not in any kind of physical discomfort, well furnished with money, but prevented from any external contact with, or participation in the affairs of the kingdom.

These 'ambas' are a striking feature of the plateau country. They are usually the isolated peak at the end of

[1] Ibid.   [2] Ibid.

4

a chain of mountains which jut out into the desert, or into the deep ravines by which the country is intersected by its great river systems. The climate of these high regions is extremely healthy; they are well watered, and though the sun is hot the air is perpetually cool and fresh. In the valleys on the other hand are mosquitoes and malaria, snails and bilharzia, and all the other unpleasant accompaniments of the tropical low country.

Little wonder that the ruling race kept to their highlands where agriculture was easy and the three months of the rainy season never failed to fill up spring and stream, and so ensure rich pasture for their animals and fuel and food for themselves.

With the rise of Islam, and the subsequent occupation first of Palestine and later of Egypt by the Arabs, Ethiopia was cut off from contact with the Christian civilization of Europe, and her history is lost to us. We know that during the twelfth and thirteenth centuries a dynasty not of Solomonian descent occupied the throne, and that one of these kings, Lalibela, was the reputed builder of the famous rock churches in Lasta, where he established his capital which bears his name. His memory is reverenced and he is regarded as a saint by the Ethiopian Church. But we know little of the historical facts of these two centuries, and it is only with the return to power of the Solomonian line in the person of Amda Seyum that the story begins to take shape historically in the chronicles that began to be written in the fourteenth century by the king's scribe.

It was during the twelfth century in Europe that mysterious stories began to spread about a Christian monarch who lived and ruled somewhere in the East. Many fabulous tales were related of his power and wealth, and during the centuries that saw the last of the Crusades there was always a hope that this Christian king would come to attack the Moslems from the rear. When, however, this failed to occur and no trace could be found in Asia of a king to justify these stories, men began to look for him elsewhere. When explorers sent out by Henry the Navigator reported the existence of a Christian king in Africa, opinion began to identify him with Prester John, and expeditions were sent to locate him.

The Portuguese were therefore the first Europeans to make close contact with the medieval civilization of Ethiopia, and from the fifteenth century onwards the history of the country can be traced with comparative accuracy. Alvarez, who acted as chaplain to a mission sent to investigate the country in 1520, during the reign of Lebna Dengel (or David), brought back a clear picture of the condition of the country and the magnificent, if primitive state of its rulers:

> We found a large and rich dais of very splendid carpets . . . and there we saw Prester John sitting on a platform of six steps very richly adorned. He had on his head a high crown of gold and silver, and a silver cross in his hand: there was a piece of blue taffeta before his face which covered his mouth and beard. . . . At his right hand he had a page with a silver cross in his hand. The Prester was dressed in a rich robe of brocade and a silk shirt of wide sleeves which looked like a pelisse.

Most of the information about the country at that time comes from the same source.

During the sixteenth century the kingdom was still divided into a number of tributary kingdoms, though these had for the most part been reduced to the rank of provinces, ruled over by governors, rather than kings. Even those who still retained this title were selected and supervised by the King of Kings. Some of these tributaries were Moslem as well as Christian and it seems to have been quite possible for the Christian monarch to have chosen his wife at times from among the daughters of these subject kings of another faith, though the queen would then be expected to adopt the faith of her husband.

This may have led to the wars which Alvarez recounts to have taken place between the Christians and Moslems in the reign of Lebna Dengel; and these were followed by the far more serious invasion by Ahmed Gran, King of Adel in Somaliland, and his followers. Assisted by the Turks, who were now a power in the Red Sea, and furnished by them with the first match-locks ever seen in that part of the world, the armies of Islam overran almost the whole of the Christian kingdom. The churches and monasteries were ransacked and burnt, and the great majority of the people wavered in their faith before the onslaught of the infidel. The princes of the Solomonian line were massacred, and at last only the king with a small band of faithful followers, retreating before their pursuers into their strongholds among the hills, were left to defend the Christian faith.

In this calamity the king turned towards his Portuguese friends. The son of the great Vasco da Gama arrived with help—both men and guns—and within a year Ahmed Gran, who had reached as far north as Lake Tsana, was shot and his armies dispersed, though in this fighting the Portuguese leader had himself been killed. The defeat of the Moslem invaders was, however, complete; the Christian king drove south to regain his kingdom and even extended his conquests to include the former provinces of Bali and Doaro, but one loss he never regained; Massowah was seized by the Turks and Ethiopia was denied access to the sea.

The next two centuries are almost wholly taken up by various civil wars and religious wars which resulted from the advent to the country of Jesuit missions. It is not until the seventeenth century that we find the royal power successfully re-established by Basilidas, who built the new royal city of Gondar, north of Lake Tsana. This remained the capital for almost two hundred years. It was during this period that Bruce visited Ethiopia and that the first attempt at diplomatic relations with a European power was initiated. Nothing came of it, however, and during the following century the power of the kings of the Solomonian line declined, and their empire shrank within the loop of the Blue Nile. The province of Shoa to the south of Gojjam, although owing allegiance to the King of Kings, became virtually independent and had made this independence the more efficacious by setting a tribe of Galla nomads to the north, who acted as a buffer between them and the northern kingdom. Its very able governor kings achieved for it a high position of influence and importance as a barrier against the roving Moslem and Galla tribes to the east and south. It is from them that the present royal house is descended.

Meanwhile, constant intrigue and unending civil war threatened the very existence of the northern kingdom. Only one thing seemed to remain constant and unchanged— the Church with its many priests, monks, and monasteries. Yet the figurehead of the monarchy remained. Even when impotent to curb the quarrelsome nobles, when the power in his hands was at its lowest ebb, he was treated with ceremony and reverence for his person; meanwhile his unruly subjects vied with each other to achieve the hegemony for themselves and the puppet emperors whom they supported.

The decline of the empire was complete some twenty-five years before Sahle Selassie, King of Shoa, emerged into history in 1813.

2

The Family

THE present Empire of Ethiopia is divided into provinces, and a glance at the map will show that Shoa holds the central position. Cut off from the northern territory, perhaps deliberately, as has already been shown, by allowing the penetration of Galla tribes as well as by the configuration of the country itself, the rulers in Shoa, crowned on their circular hill of Mona Gasha—still a landmark on the horizon west of Addis Ababa—had established for themselves a position of considerable influence.

Deriving descent from the Solomonian line through Abatu Ya'Ihkob, a son of Lebna Dengel (or David), who had been emperor during the sixteenth century, they now began to assume a position of equality with the rulers of the north, and even to conduct negotiations and enter into relations with foreign countries. In 1840 and 1841 King Sahle Selassie received the missions of M. Rochet d'Héricourt from France, and of Major Cornwallis Harris from England. Both met the king in his capital at Ankober. 'Sahle Selassie was seated on a leathern chair, his head bare, and his hair frizzled into little curls; a small gold cross was suspended from his neck by a blue ribbon, while a "laupe" brilliantly embroidered, but partially concealed a vest of Indian workmanship embroidered with gold beneath: two massive gold bracelets on his wrists completed his costume.'[1] Under his rule Shoa enjoyed a period of peace and stable government, and

---

[1] *Abyssinia Described or the Land of Prester John*, ed. J. C. Hotten, p. 57.

Cornwallis Harris notes: 'A rich mercantile harvest is assuredly in store for those who shall unlock the portals of the Eastern Coast and shall spread navigation upon waters that have hitherto proved barren.'[1] His long reign lasted until 1847, when his son Haile Melakot succeeded him.

While Sahle Selassie ruled in Shoa there were two other powerful rulers contending for supremacy in the north— Ras Ali of Gondar (a former Moslem who had become first mayor and had then, in order to gain the support of the Church, turned Christian) and Dejazmach Wobie, who ruled supreme in the north 'from the coast of the Red Sea to Gondar,' including the whole of Tigre.

Though many travellers had visited these parts no official intercourse was maintained with any of these chiefs by the British Government until a Mr Plowden suggested to the Foreign Office the advisability of establishing a consulate at the port of Massowah, explaining how in his opinion 'a considerable commerce must ensue.'[2] On 2nd November 1848 a treaty of 'Friendship and Commerce' was concluded between England and Ras Ali, though the latter is reputed to have thought that little could ever come of it. It would seem curious that within a decade two missions should have been dispatched on similar errands to two different rulers— one of Shoa and one of Gondar—but it serves to show the confused state of affairs, both in Ethiopia itself and in the eyes of the outside world.

Ras Ali, who was not of the Solomonian line of descent, found it hard to maintain his position as head of the government and was finally killed after an engagement against a rival chief, Kassa, who had denounced his authority. This Kassa was ultimately crowned in 1855 as the Emperor Theodore. He was not, and did not claim to be, of the Solomonian line, but his vigorous and successful campaigns

[1] Ibid., p. 77.   [2] Ibid., p. 113.

H.I.M. the Emperor, eleven years old, with his father,
Ras Makonnen

in all parts of the country, and his championship of the Church, led to a general recognition of his position; he was at the outset of his career a man of strong character, imbued with an enthusiasm for Christianity and a real desire for reform. In this he failed to find support among the local chiefs, who saw only a possible check on their own freedom of action. Yet, in spite of growing unpopularity, he did much to unify the country, especially in the north. He was then strong enough to challenge the growing power of the Shoan kingdom, now under the rule of Haile Melakot, son of Sahle Selassie. He seized his capital of Ankober, and when the king died on the eve of battle, captured and imprisoned his son Menelek, then a boy of twelve years of age.

His newly unified empire had, however, no solid foundations. Disaffection and rebellion among the chiefs and governors of provinces angered and embittered the Emperor: his enthusiasm for the Church waned, his need of money entailed heavy exactions from his subjects, his cordiality and courtesy—recorded by his European friends on their first contacts with him—gave way to suspicion, malevolence, and finally madness. Venting this upon all and sundry he imprisoned and ill-treated English and other residents, thus bringing upon himself retaliatory action from the British Government, who sent a force of 16,000 men to rescue their nationals. Theodore, on the defeat of his army at Magdala in 1868, shot himself.

It was at this juncture that the young Menelek escaped and re-established himself as King of Shoa. After Tekla Giorghis had reigned for three years, Dejazmach Kassa of Tigre assumed the royal title and was crowned as the Emperor John at Axum in 1872. The latter consolidated the conquests of Theodore and added to them the important town of Harar in the south-east, which had been evacuated by the Egyptians who had held the province for ten years.

Unfortunately the good promise of his reign was cut short by his death in battle against the dervishes, who were threatening invasion from the west.

As he lay dying he called to him his son Mangasha and appointed him his heir. But Menelek, King of Shoa, had also proclaimed himself emperor, and Mangasha was not strong enough to oppose him. Menelek was regarded with favour by a large following of chiefs, as well as by the Italians, who had gained, by this time, a footing on the Eritrean coast, and were ready to put arms at his disposal in order to establish themselves as the supporters and protectors of the young Emperor. The treaty of Ucciali was signed between Menelek and his Italian allies in 1888—a treaty which appeared to the Italians to constitute an Italian protectorate over Ethiopia, but which Menelek viewed from quite a different angle; though quite willing to make use of Italian help to gain his own ends, he had no intention of becoming their tool.

Much might be written about his reign: how he extended and consolidated the work of his predecessors in the making of the Ethiopian Empire; how he set it upon the map of the world. He was no longer the mythical Prester John of medieval times, but a monarch who opened his capital to foreign legations, constructed the railway line which linked his domain with the sea, built the 'new flower' (Addis Ababa), which became the centre of trade and the seat of settled government, and noticed with favour and approval the growth and development of outstanding qualities in a young boy—the son of an old friend and able general—who was just emerging into manhood. He himself had no such son.

Sahle Selassie, King of Shoa, had a large family of sons and daughters, of whom Haile Melakot, the eldest, succeeded him. Among his daughters was one Tenagne Worq, married to

Dejazmach Walda Mikhail of Shoa-Doba. His father was Walda Melakot, a well-known figure at Sahle Selassie's court, famous as a maker of roads. Their younger son, Ras Makonnen, was therefore first cousin to the Emperor Menelek. While the latter was engaged in the wars, first within his own territories, which resulted in the unification of his empire, and then outside its boundaries, this Ras Makonnen was his able general and loyal friend. He fought at Adowa with conspicuous bravery; with his imperial master he achieved the pacification of Harar province, and put into practice such reform in the administration and in the law-courts that 'The Justice of Ras Makonnen' became a byword in his province.

When at last the Empire was consolidated from within and protected from without it was Ras Makonnen who was sent by Menelek to make friendly contacts with other nations of the world. He had visited France, Italy, and England as the emissary of the Emperor, in order to help Ethiopia to a place of respect and acknowledgment among the nations of the world; and it was perhaps these contacts with the civilizations of the West that warned and advised the Ras that without education Ethiopia could never hold her own in the world of the twentieth century.

Certain it is that it was in the atmosphere of enlightenment and reform that Ras Makonnen set himself to the administration of the rich province that, after its conquest, he was set to govern. The registration of land was his first concern, in order to facilitate the collection of government taxes. During the previous governorship of the Emir Abdullah a great many of the peasant owners had been expropriated by the local chiefs, who relied on the support that they had afforded to the late governor to confirm them in their illegal occupation. Emboldened by the reputation for justice which the new governor inspired the peasants presented their case, and after little deliberation Makonnen gave orders that they were to be reinstated in their original properties. He thus bound to him by ties of gratitude many thousands of cultivators who saw in him a protector as much as a governor.

Stories are told of his impartial justice to Ethiopian and foreigner alike. An Ethiopian who had insulted a foreigner in his shop to the point when the latter, exasperated, had beaten him up, was ordered to be imprisoned for having himself been the cause of the incident. An Austrian house-wife had trouble with her cook. The Ras ordered her to attend the court, but she asked to be excused until a time later in the day. Notwithstanding her protests the soldiers brought her by force, but were sternly reprimanded for having refused to listen to a legitimate excuse. A foreigner who had a case against a blacksmith was awarded a decision in his favour. Not content with the punishment of a fine inflicted by the Ras, the foreigner sought to have the prisoner turned out of the town. 'In our country,' said the Ras, 'we have need of every available merchant and above all of artisans. You have obtained justice, there is to be no question of expulsion.' [1]

Such stories serve to show reasons for the honour and affection in which Ras Makonnen was held both among his own people and the foreign community. Further, we have an example of his generous nature, when having himself ordered the expulsion of a foreigner convicted of murder, who had already served a long sentence in prison, he paid the passage money necessary to ensure his return to his own country.

A description of the hospitality accorded by him to foreign visitors may be found in many of the books written by visitors to the country in the last decade of the nineteenth century.

[1] Adrien Zervos: *L'Empire d'Ethiopie.*

Ras Makonnen's house in Harar

Carved doorway of Ras Makonnen's house.
The inscription above the door reads:
'Dejazmach Tafari lived here'

'We pitched our camp at the required spot, a slight rise in the grassy level overlooking a marsh, with a clear stream half a mile off, and found a plenteous offering of bread and sheep and tej sent by Ras Makonnen . . .' and after meeting him: 'Ras Makonnen had produced on us a pleasing impression. He is a small dark man with delicate hands, large expressive eyes, a small black beard and moustache, and a most intelligent cast of countenance. His voice is very gentle and his manners extremely dignified and quiet. What he said was little but to the point, and he gave us then and thereafter the impression of a man who wielded a good deal of power in a quiet way.'[1]

Monseigneur Jarosseau, who spent his long life in Ethiopia and the greater part of it in Harar province, writes thus of him: 'Makonnen, justly admired as the greatest military leader that Abyssinia has perhaps ever known, as the victor of Adowa, respected on all sides for his high intelligence and his uprightness, was also much beloved for his justice and goodness, and his spiritual character.'[2]

He married Waizero Yeshimabeit in 1875. She was the daughter of a chieftain of the Wollo country north-east of Addis Ababa. Its people are among the hardiest and most hard working in the empire, for their cold bleak country is a good preparation for courage and endurance. Of this Church union were born ten children. Yet the only child to survive of this large family was the present Emperor. How precious then must have been this youngest born; what hopes must have rested on him; in what full measure has he repaid the love and care which was to prepare him to serve his country and the whole world.

Tafari Makonnen was born in his father's country home near Harar on 23rd July 1892 (16th Hamle 1884 in the

[1] Gleichen: *With the Mission to Menelik*, p. 40.
[2] Gaetan Bernoville: *Monseigneur Jarosseau*, p. 231.

Ethiopian calendar).   He was baptized in Harar at the church which his father had built and received his Christian name of Haile Selassie. As very often happens in Ethiopian families he was called at home by another name, Tafari.

3

The Country and its People

AT this stage some description of the country and
its people may not come amiss to the general
reader to serve as a background to the story of the
life of its remarkable ruler. So much has changed in the
life of the town dweller in Addis Ababa in the short space of
the Emperor's own life that it is difficult to visualize the
simplicity and comparative lack of material comfort in which
he grew up and passed the early days of his public life.

Yet the life of the countryside has changed little—the
climate, the seasons, the vastness and beauty of the mountain
scenery, the hardship of travel on foot or by mule in the heat
of the coastal plains or lowland valley, these remain the
same as they have been for many centuries, and it may serve
to give some idea of the activities and, at many times, the
rigours of his early years. A friendly visit to our English
farm, some thirty miles from the capital, in 1925, entailed a
six o'clock start by mule over the mountain barrier of
Entotto—10,000 feet above sea level—a gallop over the
plains on a spirited Arab stallion, to accomplish the journey
in four or five hours; the afternoon was spent in a tour, still
on horseback, extending some three or four miles; and the
Regent rode back by the same route and in the same way
next day. That visit was for friendship and pleasure; but it
was only one of many other journeys undertaken under less
pleasant conditions and for less friendly purposes.

The plateau which constitutes by far the greater part of
Ethiopia stands embattled by its great escarpment east, north,

and south in the midst of the low country—desert on three sides; and on the west, where there is a gentler, more sloping descent from the high country, lies the hot humid Nile basin. The whole empire, with its federated territory of Eritrea—the size of Germany and France together—covers over 400,000 square miles, of which a great part is uncultivatable desert. Narrowing at its northern extremity to a strip only a few miles wide, where the western edge of the Rift Valley nears the coast of the Red Sea the desert widens out farther south to include the Danakil and Aussa country. This lies to the north of the railway which runs along the hills which form a spur of the Eastern Escarpment. South of these again lies the great stretch of the Ogaden—now lately restored to Ethiopian control—arid plains sloping slowly to the sea, over which the Somali tribes have wandered for centuries with their flocks and herds of camels.

Still farther south the Boran country spreads out north of the Kenya frontier.

The plateau country stands one compact solid block, scarred by the deep ravines of the three great river systems. One spur only extends from the main block eastward toward the Somaliland frontier and on the last ridges of this stands the town of Harar, capital of the province of that name, and for the last fifty years bound by special ties of loyalty and affection to the royal family. The railway, which lies thirty miles north of the town, runs along the foot-hills until, crossing the Hawash river where it debouches on to the plains of the Danakil country, it climbs up the western rim of the Rift Valley. Where the volcanic lava flow from Mt Fautalle spreads over the plain it works its way up the 6,000-foot escarpment, past the crater lakes of the Bishoftu hills, to emerge into the 8,000-foot level of Addis Ababa itself. The city lies encircled by the same circular ridge of the Entoto hills over which the car road to the Blue Nile and

the north now winds its way—a road holding memories of
the Emperor's return to his capital in May 1941.

The traveller of to-day who reaches Addis Ababa by plane
from any direction, for the airport outside the town is now
the centre of a network of routes, has little idea of
the difficulties that had to be overcome in the old days by
whatever route the early adventurer, soldier or trader,
entered.

In florid style Major Cornwallis describes the type of
desert country across which his caravan worked its way
towards Sahle Selassie's capital of Ankober.

A suffocating Pandemonium where no zephyr fanned the
fevered skin; where the furnace-like vapour exhaled almost chok-
ing respiration, created an indomitable thirst, and not the smallest
shade or shelter existed.   Each weary hour brought a grievous
accession, but no alleviation, to the fearful torments.[1]

Any overland approach to the plateau must then be made
through regions of intense heat, whether over the dry
scorching sands of the desert or through the sweltering heat
of the Nile tributary valleys.   So grew the idea in old days
that Ethiopia was a land of tropical heat; but the popular
idea of the climate was neither flattering nor true.   Although
the whole country is only a few degrees north of the equator,
on the upland plateaus with an average height of 8,000 feet
the air is perpetually cool, even at midday, and the nights
can be bitterly cold.   From September to May the mornings
are like a fresh day in June in England, only in the rainy
season between June and September do the clouds sweep over
the hills in a fine Scotch mist that can be quite as cold and
penetrating as its counterpart in the British Isles.   The sun
at midday is hot but one cannot sit without a jersey in the
shade.   Nine months of the year are comparatively dry—

[1] *Abyssinia Described*, pp. 18, 19.

too dry for sensitive skins—but the months between June and September are those of the 'big rains,' which are more or less heavy every day, and which fill spring and ditch and dike and river in an extraordinarily short time.

The feast of 'Maskal,' or the Finding of the True Cross, which comes at the end of September, coincides with the end of the rains, and usually there is no heavy rain after that date. Rivers and streams fall from raging torrents to fordable streams. Crops are harvested: the hay is cut, barley in November, wheat in December, tef (fine millet from which the bread is usually made) in January. With the advent of 'small rains' in February (though they are not completely regular) the hard dry ground is softened again, enough to allow the primitive plough to work. Thus in the normal year the climate provides ideal conditions for successful but not too exacting agriculture.

While on the plateau itself this temperate climate prevails, in the deep valleys cut by the three great rivers and their tributaries the heat is tropical and the humidity considerable. Within a few miles one can pass from the ice of the upland stream and cutting winds of the plateau to the heat of the African jungle with its palms and tree ferns, to take a dip in the warmth of the river pools, whose water flows down to the Blue Nile. These great chasms in the volcanic crust of the plateau are from two to four thousand feet deep, and climate and animal and vegetable life are as different as if one had stepped into another continent.

The geography of the country has naturally moulded its history; and the diversity of the land itself, with its burning deserts, its complex mountain ranges and river chasms, its variety of temperature and climate, has helped to produce the same diversity among its inhabitants. It has endowed them with qualities of vigour and self-reliance, of independence and self-assertion, and at the same time the

Kurt Schumacher

Harar, a walled city seen from the hills, looking south, with Mount Kondudo in the background

corresponding drawbacks of lack of cohesion and co-operation, of over-confidence and arrogance.

These features of character true of centuries of her history are equally true of Ethiopia to-day. There are over thirty languages, exclusive of dialects, spoken among all the peoples of the empire; and though the Government is trying by its educational policy of one language of instruction to unify this medley of peoples, there are of course many other differences of tradition, religion, and custom which will long preserve their local independence.

We may, however, consider four main divisions of the people, of which the first, the Amharas, were the dominant race, whose language Amharic is rapidly becoming universal, as that of the Emperor and his court. Their Christian religion has marked them out through the centuries as distinct from all other African peoples, and is indeed the cause of much of their strange history. They inhabit the northern provinces of the empire: Tigre, Amhara, Gojjam, and part of Shoa, an area equal to about one-third of the country.

To the south and west of this Amhara bloc live the Gallas, invaders from the south who overran the country during the sixteenth century and settled in it, only to be reconquered themselves in successive wars, and finally incorporated in the empire by Menelek. They had by then extended towards the north, driving a wedge between the Amhara and the Danakil. Their powerful king, Negus Mikhail, was one of the chief generals in both King John's army against the dervishes and Menelek's army at the battle of Adowa. But, though in origin and language a distinct racial type, there is no political cohesion among the Gallas. During the past five hundred years indeed the forces of both war and peace have been welding Galla and Amhara into a unity which comprises all the people of the highlands, who are agriculturists by nature and by circumstance; and it would

now be difficult to draw any separate line, whether political
or geographical, to separate them.

Among other inhabitants of the highlands must be mentioned the Guragies; the strongest physically among the
different tribes who live south-west of the capital, they come
up for long periods to do the hardest manual labour and are
often employed as gardeners and woodmen. They have a
special skill in the preparation of ground for forestry and are
then employed when the eucalyptus forest is ready for
timber, in cutting and carting. Sir Charles Rey in his book
on Abyssinia [1] advances the interesting theory that these
people, living by themselves in a small district between the
road to Jimma and the great lakes, are the descendants of a
colony of European slaves, planted there by Egyptians in far
off times to work the copper mines which existed there.
They speak their own language and are partly Mohammedans;
but in the war of 1935–6 they fought well for the empire
against the Italians.

Another group must be mentioned—the distinction
again being one of religion as well as of race. The Falasha
or Ethiopian Jews live in the district round the highest
mountains of Ethiopia which lies north-west of Lake Tsana.
Numerically small, their prowess at one time as fighters was
considerable, and they even seized and held the throne for
a period. They still practise the Jewish religion with all
its rites and ceremonies, and some of their own as well,
but it is interesting to note that they know no Hebrew, and
that their scriptures are in the Geez language of the Ethiopian Church. They are manual workers, chiefly smiths and
workers in iron, and they live in their own communities;
though they come from the north they can be found all over
the country. They look upon themselves as Jewish exiles,
and a return to the Promised Land is part of their religion;

[1] Sir Charles Rey: *Unconquered Abyssinia.*

but they are believed to be non-Semitic in origin, though the name Falasha means exile, and they are of different extraction from the other peoples of the plateau, being probably of Cushite descent.

The third large class comprises the desert people of the east, the Danakil, and of the south-east, the many tribes of the Somali. Entirely different in origin, features, customs, and habits of daily life from the peoples of the plateau, these nomads pursue their own way unheeded and unchecked. Both men and women, with their spare and graceful figures, are quite unlike their more sturdy and stouter compatriots of the plateau. Their camel caravans may often be seen from the railway lurching through the stony deserts of Gildessa, the lank forms of the Somali tribesmen plodding beside them; the Somali women with their print dresses and scarlet wraps, bent under their burdens, but stepping out, as only nomad women can do, to cover the miles that stretch between one camping ground and the next. It seems inconceivable that human beings can live their life out in such a waste country and under a burning sky. The tents are made of camels' hair fabric stretched on a wicker-work frame and everything rolls up easily, to make a cumbrous yet not a heavy load. It was the friction over the water rights of these people that set the spark, rigorously fanned by Italians, to the Italo-Ethiopian war.

The population of these regions is of course very sparse, and the Somalis' northern neighbours the Danakil are, except in the Bati market or on the Assab road, far less visible and accessible. One may occasionally see a warrior, leaning on his spear, naked save for the girdle at his waist, contemplating the train as it lumbers by—perhaps reckoning the number of spear heads to a length of rail, for depredations on the railway line for this purpose have often been reported. Their country is divided into districts rul d over by their

Sultans, and their yearly tribute is remitted regularly to the Government treasury.

There remains one great group of peoples. Conveniently called 'Shankalla,' they are the real blacks of the warmer hills and valleys in western Ethiopia that slope down from the plateau country into the White Nile basin. They are people of innumerable different tribes—speaking different and little known-tongues, devoid of political purpose or unity, the prey, through their paganism, ignorance, and lack of co-operation, of the more closely confederated highland tribes; and possessed of a docility and also, perhaps as a result of centuries of slave raiding, of an apathy that is hard to awaken to action. They not only failed to combine but they carried on their own quarrels regardless of their danger, raiding for cattle and slaves among themselves, and laying themselves open as an easy prey to the slave trader. For the bribe of a few rifles he would acquire the victims he desired, and then move on to the next tribe to carry on the same business.

Here then are the varied constituents of the Ethiopian Empire, named not inaptly by the Arabs who came into contact with them 'the medley,' and as far back as the Old Testament the 'mingling of the peoples.' Over them all the great Menelek established his authority, so that even now to swear 'by Menelek' is to pledge an oath. He conquered them, converted them, and combined them into an empire. Who would answer the challenge to govern this empire when its founder died and his successor betrayed his trust?

4

Birth and Early Life

THE rains had begun in Harar that July day—great clouds were again massing on flat-topped Kondudu. A few miles out from the town the Governor had his country villa at Ejarsa Gore on the Kombolcha road, a wattle and daub house with a certain Indian appearance about its outside veranda. The forecourt was crowded with guests from near and far.

When a woman is in travail, other women will go to her and salute her, saying: 'Didst thou pass the night well? May Mary keep near thee!' When the travail is over they will wish her well, saying: 'May Mary restore thee with honour.' Then, when the child is born the women may raise the cry of joy.

The glad father will fire his rifle, if such is found, and drawing his sword will stretch it across the door for a space, while the old women raise up the babe to watch it. Before an hour has passed one will have placed butter in his mouth, and the mother will lie tight swathed in a length of cloth, lest her back ail her. 'But Mary is hearkening, nor will she need much aid.' [1]

Some such scene we can imagine in that country house near Harar. The arrival of woman after woman to give her loyal greeting, and to gather round the mother's bed to discuss how soon the babe will be born and to give sympathy, encouragement, and help.

After some weeks comes the ceremony of baptism. In the Ethiopian Church the babies are brought to the church in the very early morning if it be on a Sunday, so that, as

[1] Walker: *The Abyssinian at Home*, p. .

soon as the actual baptism is over, they may receive their first communion. The name is given four times over by the priest: at the revolving, when the child is turned to the four points of the compass; at the aspersion with holy water, after the words: 'I baptize thee for the Father, for the Son, and for the Holy Ghost'; at the tying of the neck cord of five cotton threads which all Christians wear; and at the anointing, when the babe is anointed on forehead, cheek, chin, and breast. Then the child is carried by the deacon to the priest, who will place in his mouth the consecrated bread dipped in the wine. Then the godfather takes the child again and restores him to his mother and they go home.

A male child is raised up to Christianity on the fortieth day, a girl on the eightieth. Twenty months later, on 14th March 1894 (Amharic date 5th Megabit 1886), Waizero Yeshimabeit died in childbirth—and the child Tafari was left to the care of his father.

The houses of even the great men of that period were far from luxurious. Though fine carpets and rugs have always been in the possession of the nobility—and frequently carried about with them when they were in camp, or moving from one country house to another—their houses were usually empty of much other furniture than tables and chairs. The baby would be handed over to some of the many women servants of the household, and much care would be taken to see that he was safeguarded from too much exposure to the sun: he would be kept mostly indoors, and carefully veiled when taken outside.

There is no mention of the small boy having been seen when Count Gleichen writes his description of the arrival of the Mission to Menelek in 1897. They visited Ras Makonnen in Harar:

Then through more narrow streets [he writes], lined with

soldiery, till at last we drew rein and turned our mules up a couple of steps into the narrow courtyard of Makonnen's house. Here there was once more a guard of honour for us, dark warriors with rifle and silver shield, dressed in cloaks and silks of all colours of the rainbow. Up the wooden stairs and on the landing there were more of them coiffed with a strip of lion's mane to denote their valour, and then—we found ourselves in a little room, so dark after the sunlight without that at first we could hardly distinguish Ras Makonnen sitting by the window, and pointing graciously to eight cane chairs arranged along the walls.[1]

So even if there was no luxury in his upbringing the child would from the first be accustomed to the pomp and ceremonial attached to his father's position. The natural dignity of his own carriage may well have been founded in these early days, when a child notices and remembers everything.

His first lessons in the Amharic script and language would surely be in his own home, where the 'confessor' of the household, Aba Walda Kidan, or some priest closely connected with the family, would teach him to read. Every Christian family in Ethiopia had this confessor, or 'soul father' as his title goes, and early religious instruction would naturally come from him. Ras Makonnen was present at the coronation of King Edward VII as representative of the Emperor Menelek, and this visit abroad had strengthened his conviction that education was an absolute essential to the progress of his country. He applied it to the upbringing of his son, now a boy of ten. On his return in September 1902 he arranged that Lij Tafari should begin lessons in French with a Dr Vitalien, a native of Guadaloupe whom he had himself brought to Harar to open the hospital which bears his name. But as he was a very busy man the doctor could not spend more than an hour a day with the young boy, and so Ras Makonnen asked Aba Andreas (later Monseigneur

[1] Op. cit., p. 45.

Jarosseau) of the French Mission in Harar to send him a young lad who was well educated and could speak French, to act as companion tutor to his son. Aba Samuel was chosen and was engaged by Ras Makonnen for this purpose. He proved an excellent choice. Meanwhile in the house Lij Tafari would be under the care of his guardian Fitaurari Quollach. In his father's absence Fitaurari Banti, Ras Makonnen's deputy, would also be responsible for the boy's safe keeping. His companions during these years were his cousin Imeru Haile Selassie, later to become Ras, and Tafari Belaw. Lij Tafari remained at Harar under instruction for the next five years, though we hear of a visit to Addis Ababa with his father in 1903 when the Emperor Menelek expressed a wish to see the boy. A few years afterwards he created him a Dejazmach (November 1905).

So passed his early life until his father's death in April 1906 when Dejazmach Tafari was thirteen years old. Ras Makonnen was on his way up to Addis Ababa and was at his country house at Kolobi when he was taken ill and died after a few days' illness. Bishop Jarosseau speaks of the general grief and sense of loss, of how many of the nobles arrived, surrounded the young Prince Tafari who was there, kissing his hand, his head, his feet. He was actually governor of the district, for just before his death his father had raised him to the rank of Governor and the title of Dejazmach then given him by Ras Makonnen was later confirmed by Menelek, together with an appointment as Governor of Solali. At the same time Ras Makonnen appointed him his heir, despite the fact that there was an elder son by a former marriage.

He was, however, too young to be in charge of so large and rich a province as Harar, which a little later was given to the elder brother, just mentioned. Dejazmach Tafari himself was summoned to Addis Ababa by the Emperor Menelek, who had seen the rare qualities of the boy. Here he lived, as so many of the young nobles did in medieval England, the life of an esquire at the Court, watching the routine of the Court, hearing the talk on men and politics, picking up the latest information on the affairs internal and external of the realm.   On the other side they also could be watched, their character estimated, their abilities tested. He was appointed Governor of Solali in May 1906 and a year later Governor of Ba'Aso.

So the boy found himself in the midst of men and affairs— to earn at once the attention and approval of the ageing Emperor.   For the latter detected in the son those abilities which he had tested and valued in the father.   The result was that the young Dejazmach found himself sent back to school to further his education, and enrolled in the new Menelek School which had been founded in the city and put in charge of an Egyptian, Hanna Bey Saleb, while his province was governed by proxy.   He remained there for the next three years, when at the age of seventeen he held his first real office.   Speaking many years later of this first secular school to be founded he has said:

The Emperor Menelek II after ruling for many years in accordance with the traditions of our country, on initiating relations with foreign states recognized that the educational system of our country was insufficient and that it was necessary to bring it into line with theirs.   He therefore established this school to meet the immediate need for foreign languages.   As an example to the clergy and people he caused all the boys who had, as relatives and connections of his, been brought up at the palace, to enter this school.   I myself was one of the boys who were there at the start, when this school was founded.[1]

[1] *Speeches of H.I.M. Haile Selassie I*, Part I, 21 July 1927.

5

Taking the Lead

I T was when he left school when he was barely seventeen years old that the Emperor Menelek gave him his first real governorship—that of the rich province of Sidamo—in April 1909.

In order to understand the life and work of a Governor in a distant province in those days, it is necessary to know something of the life and ways of the country people among whom his work lay, and of the problems, military, legal and administrative, commercial and agricultural, with which he would be expected to deal, for the office of Governor covered all these duties.

Sidamo is one of the richest provinces in the empire. Lying at an altitude of about 6,000 feet, it is a fertile and well-watered country; the streams flowing down from the mountains on the west flow into Lake Abaya, and on the south-east there is another series of streams that later join the Ganale Doria. Coffee, cereals, and timber are its chief products. Recollections of a journey through part of the province are of wide open pastures and arable land, and as the road wound up and down the hills that form the backbone of the province, of pleasant forest glades of podocarpus, olive, and blackwood. The houses are largely constructed of bamboo stalks and are surrounded each by their own plantation of *musa ensete* and coffee-trees. Much also of the coffee is wild, and grows in the shade of the forest trees. The fibre of the *musa ensete* is now a valuable product, and though it has always been the custom for the Sidamo peoples to plant it round their houses, for they use the root to make bread, the rising value of its fibre on the Addis Ababa market has greatly encouraged its production. The population of the province is very varied as there are a great many different Sidamo peoples, which only half a century ago ruled themselves in comparative independence with their own 'Balabats' or chieftains.

Here then Dejazmach Tafari found himself at the age of seventeen ready to put into practice those reforms that he had already seen at work in his father's governorate. Land registration followed the footsteps of the young man as he went from village to village assessing and collecting the dues that came to him.

He would have maintained an armed body of men, professional soldiers, who would accompany him as he rode on his richly caparisoned mule from place to place. He would be attended by his secretaries, his treasurer, his officers, civil and military; he would expect, as he made his circuit round his province, that all these attendants would be fed and housed by the people of the villages through which he passed. His business would be varied: the maintenance of law and order—for there was no established police force in those days—the administration of justice in those cases where there were appeals from the lower courts to that of the Governor; and this would probably be carried out in the open air at some suitable and customary place. He would sit there, his officials standing around him, his escort in the background, a ceremonial carpet thrown down for his chair, which would be carried behind him wherever he went— possibly a gaily embroidered Indian umbrella over his head and a slave with a fly whisk hovering alongside him. He would listen to the impassioned prosecutor as he waved his arms, with his *shamma*—a long white 'toga,' usually homespun of Ethiopian cotton, about 4 yards long and 1½ yards wide—wound round him in a ceremonial way; witness after witness would step out of the ring of the attentive crowd, to give his evidence as melodramatically as possible. Judgment must be given; there is no coded law to help him, only a wealth of tradition and precedent that he must follow. He may seek counsel of the old men of the district 'the elders,' who will sit with him, as we may picture them, to help him give sentence; and when given, he will leave the execution of the sentence in the hands of the local chief, while he passes on to hear the assessments made in the district (which he will probably ride round and see for himself) of the Government tax which must be paid in kind.

He will ride in through the market, where the whole chattering crowd will rise as one man to bow as he passes by; he will stop to inquire about market dues, to receive reports of produce and prices. As he rides on, a man will run up with a stone on his shoulder and fling himself down with the cry 'Abet, Abet'—some grievance, some claim to be heard. He will stop to listen, call one of his officers to leave in his hands an investigation into the merits of the case, which will be put before him later. And all this goes on daily, in a province as large as Belgium—hundreds of miles— and that means days or weeks of travel, away from the centre of government. He has the responsibility of keeping his soldiers contented, the countryside quiet, justice maintained, prosperity ensured, so that the Emperor in far-off Addis Ababa may have a good opinion of the young man to whom he has entrusted so much responsibility. And he receives no salary, his officers and soldiers no pay—that must come, willingly or unwillingly, from the people over whom he is set. If they get too little his army is discontented—if they get too much it means the country is plundered and impoverished as in the old feudal days of England. And the Government must receive its dues in grain and cattle, honey

and coffee—the more that comes, the more the Emperor in
Addis Ababa will think of his young Governor.

Some weeks of this life show him his province—his duties
and responsibilities.   Then he goes back to his provincial
capital with knowledge of his people and their ways, their
problems and possibilities, before him.   Here there will be
religious duties as well, for the Church and its priests are a
powerful influence in the country; and further, he himself
has a profound religious feeling that his upbringing and his
education have implanted and fostered, and that has been
later so much in evidence in his life.   And feast and fast days
are numerous and must be observed with all the time and
ritual that is demanded by them.

He had little more than eighteen months in Sidamo, but
in that short time he began to create for himself the reputation of being a young man quite out of the ordinary—
beginning to put into practice the first principles of good
government which his father's teaching and practice had
instilled into him.

In 1907 his elder half-brother, to whom the coveted
heritage of Harar had been granted on Ras Makonnen's death,
fell ill and died.   The province was transferred to Dejazmach Balcha from 1909 to 1911.   Dejazmach Tafari was
appointed as Governor and Balcha returned to Sidamo.
When the appointment was made he handed over his province, and made his way back via Addis Ababa to his birth-
place and his own people.

At once he began with immense energy, and with the
useful experience that he had now gained, to thrash out for
himself methods of administration suited to the country's
needs at its stage of development at that time, dealing in turn
with security, justice, and administration.   He had five
years in which to put these into practice—an experience that
was to stand him in good stead when later on, as Regent, he

began his programme of the inauguration of 'model provinces.'

On coming back to Harar, he installed himself in his
father's palace where he had lived as a child, picked up his
old ties of affection and friendship, and in July 1911 married.
Waizero Menan was the daughter of Janterar Asfan and
Waizero Sehin, and was through her mother the grand-
daughter of King Mikhail of Wollo. They were married in
the church which Ras Makonnen had built in Harar—a union
which through years of good and ill fortune, in times of
stress and peril, of hope and progress and discouragement,
was to prove a source of strength to Ethiopia, of great
happiness to themselves, and an object lesson to their people.
Their eldest daughter, Princess Tenagne Worq, was born in
Harar in January 1913, and their eldest son, Crown Prince
Asfa Wassen, in July 1916.

Politically these were exciting years. As far back as
May 1906—only two months after the death of Ras Makonnen, who, it was thought by many, might be nominated by
Menelek as his successor to the throne—the Emperor
Menelek had an illness, probably a slight stroke, which was
the preliminary to the long period of incapacitation which
was now to supervene. His powers rapidly declined and
from the end of 1908 he became almost wholly paralysed,
though he had periods of lucidity.

In January 1908 the Emperor Menelek had appointed
ministers to the various government departments, in order
to ease the burden on his own shoulders, which plan was
not, as might have been hoped, a successful one But in
1909, when another stroke deprived him of the power of
speech, he rallied sufficiently on 10th June to proclaim as
his heir and successor Lij Yasu, his grandson by a daughter
who had married Negus Mikhail of Wollo. At the same
time he nominated Ras Tasamma as guardian of the young

prince, who was then a boy of twelve. Ras Tasamma assumed full powers and used a seal with a lion on it and the legend 'Ras Bitwaded Tasamma Regent Plenipotentiary of the Ethiopian Realm.' But in April 1911 he was suddenly taken ill and died.

The Empress Taitu had much resented the transference of power to Ras Tasamma and tried to regain the Imperial power in March 1910, making appointments of her own choice, for the aged Emperor was entirely losing grip and the powerful Rases, who saw in the weakness of their ruler only an opportunity for their own aggrandizement, were scheming each for his own advantage. There was even a skirmish in the palace grounds between rival factions, and the dying Emperor had to be carried into the cellar for safety. Affairs rapidly fell into confusion; intrigue and self-seeking prevailed.

It was a misfortune that the Regent died thus suddenly, and that the Council of State, instead of waiting to see how the boy grew up, decided that Lij Yasu was now old enough to assume for himself the responsibilities of Regent. Despite a certain irresponsibility he was clever and intelligent, but freed from all real control he consorted with the wrong type of companion, formed dissolute habits, and offended the Council and Menelek's old officers by his arbitrary acts. Finally and most fatally he turned away from his own Church and faith, and developed leanings toward the Moslem faith.

All this the young Dejazmach Tafari watched from his governorates of Sidamo and Harar. He saw the action of the Ethiopian chiefs who in 1910 had compelled the Empress Taitu to stop interference in affairs of state and to lead a life of retirement, devoting her time to the care of her invalid husband. He saw the way of life of the young ruler and its repercussions on the people whom he governed—most of all on the nobles who had feared though half resented Menelek's nominal rule. All this time he kept out of the broil of the internal affairs of the Government, busied in his own work, consolidating his own position as a successful governor.

An incident occurred in June 1915 which has often been referred to as an omen revealing that Providence had preserved Tafari for a special role, for great tasks and achievements in the future. It has already been mentioned that out of a family of ten he was the only child to survive the perils of infancy. In a boating accident on Lake Haramaya he and two others alone escaped. In this tragic occurrence he lost his old friend and tutor Aba Samuel, a cause of great personal sorrow. 'I have lost my best friend,' he is reported to have said. 'Never shall I find another like him.' Indeed with Aba Samuel passed the last links with his home and childhood.

The outbreak of the First World War led perforce to a slackening of the interest of the European Powers in Ethiopian affairs, but it also led to an increase in internal chaos. In 1915 Lij Yasu issued a pronouncement that he was descended from the Prophet Mahomet, and he donned the Moslem turban in public. He went so far as to present the Turkish Consul-General in Harar with an Ethiopian flag on which was embroidered the crescent and the motto 'There is no God but Allah.' His intrigues with the Turkish Consul-General naturally perturbed the allies—the British, French, and Italians; but this was nothing to the scandal he caused among his own people by this renunciation of the faith they had guarded so jealously.

In the beginning of May 1916 Dejazmach Tafari was summoned to the capital by Lij Yasu. The order was peremptory and the summons seemed ominous of Lij Yasu's displeasure. He did not return, and by June it became definitely known that he had been relieved of his province and transferred to Kaffa without any of the usual forms of courtesy which accompany the transfer of a chief from one

Lovelace

View from the edge of the escarpment on the Addis Ababa-Dessis-Asmara road near Debra Sina, 125 miles north of Addis Ababa

province to another. This transfer caused considerable dissatisfaction in Harar, where Tafari was very popular, and it became clear that Lij Yasu intended to place all the power in Harar in the hands of Mohammedans. No governor was appointed to succeed Tafari, and it was understood that Lij Yasu would retain Harar as a royal reserve.

The story of an eye-witness of the events that followed is of signal interest. At the end of July 1916, Lij Yasu arrived secretly at Dire Dawa, having left Addis Ababa without giving any indication of his intentions. He arrived in this Moslem centre in time for the feast of Bairam, and celebrated the occasion by attending the mosque in person and offering prayers as a Moslem. During his short stay in Dire Dawa he carried on his intrigues with the Mohammedans in quite an open manner, and distributed to them broadcast some hundreds of rifles which he found in the customs houses. He adopted the dress of a Danakil, shaving his head and trimming his beard after the manner of that tribe.

After paying a flying visit to Djibuti, where he attempted to persuade the French authorities to supply him with arms, Lij Yasu left Dire Dawa for Jigjiga on 17th August, accompanied by a handful of Ethiopians and a large following of Somalis. At Jigjiga he appears to have ingratiated himself with the Somalis by giving them rifles, ammunition, clothing, and money.

These doings caused consternation amongst the leaders of the nation in Addis Ababa, which was not lessened by the receipt of a strong protest from the Allied Legations there, and led to the sending of priests and chiefs to Lij Yasu to point out to him the folly of his ways; but he remained indifferent and obstinate.

He arrived in Harar on 5th September and, instead of taking up his quarters at the palace there, went into residence with the Ydlibi family, Syrians, personal friends of his.

It was on 27th September 1916 that the storm broke, the day after the Maskal celebrations. On that day the Council of State and the Ethiopian chiefs took the law into their own hands. Gathering their forces together at Addis Ababa and sending a contingent of soldiery down to Harar, they declared that Lij Yasu was deposed, that Zauditu, Menelek's daughter by a former wife, was appointed Empress, and that Dejazmach Tafari—perhaps as his father's son, perhaps because he had given evidence of energy, ability, and constructive policy—should be Regent and Heir to the Throne with the title of Ras. 'We will never submit to Islam,' they declared. 'We do not wish our country to be delivered to the foreigner through the malice of Lij Yasu, who is leading our kingdom to ruin.'[1] The Abuna (Archbishop) Mattheos put the seal on this unprecedented action by declaring Lij Yasu excommunicate.

Tafari's acquiescence and lead in these events needs the following comment. He had been up to that moment, and indeed has been ever since, very careful to do nothing to impair the prestige of the throne. When in 1911 Lij Yasu was confirmed in the Regency by the Council of State he had thought it expedient to bind to his side the man whom he felt to be his most potent rival, and he had therefore made a contract on his oath with Tafari whereby he on his side engaged never to remove the latter from his governorship of Harar, while Tafari on his side promised to render him continuous and loyal support. But when Lij Yasu deposed Tafari from the governorship of Harar and transferred him to Kaffa, this automatically released Tafari from his side of the bargain, and from then onwards he felt there was no course open to him but to throw in his lot with the Shoan chiefs, whose natural leader he soon became.

On the morning of 28th September rumours began to

[1] Jones and Monroe: *Proclamation 1916*, p. 159.

fly about the town of Harar, like fire over dry stubble, that Lij Yasu had been officially deposed at the capital and Waizero Zauditu had been proclaimed Empress of Ethiopia. On the same day it became common knowledge that a telegram signed by Tafari as Ras and Regent, addressed to the Governor of Harar, instructing that chief to seize and enchain Lij Yasu, had been received at the telegraph office, but that this had been delivered into the hands of Lij Yasu himself by the official in charge of the posts and telegraphs. Immediately after this, telegraphic communication with the capital ceased, as also the postal services.

On receiving the telegram Lij Yasu summoned the leading priests in Harar and made them swear that they would ex-communicate any chiefs and soldiers who proved unfaithful to him. At the same time he swore on the Cross and Bible that he was a true Christian and remained absolutely faithful to the interests of his country. On the evening of the same day he promoted three Fitauraris to the rank of Dejazmach, and imprisoned Kagnazmach Imeru, the cousin and faithful adherent of Tafari.

On 1st October, at midday, these Dejazmaches were ordered to proceed at once with their troops to oppose the forces coming from Addis Ababa. One of them, the Syrian Ydlibi, went down to Dire Dawa and enlisted three hundred Turkish Arabs and others. In the meantime Lij Yasu remained at the palace in Harar. He was, like everyone else, without reliable news from Addis Ababa, but he must long before this have realized that he had completely lost the confidence and goodwill of his people, and that his one and faint hope lay with the Mohammedans.

By midday on 8th October it become known that Lij Yasu was leaving the town that night, which he did shortly after dusk. Before he left news was circulating in the town that the officers sent to oppose the troops that had been sent from Addis Ababa had deserted, and with their men gone over to the enemy. The night passed quietly and a tour of the town before midnight found the streets deserted except for groups of Somalis looking for a way to get out of the town. This was denied to them as the gates were closed, and they were prisoners within the walls. At daybreak the town guard lined up outside the walls, and those Somalis who attempted to scale them were shot. Inside the town those who surrendered quietly were disarmed; those who offered resistance were killed. At 11 a.m. a stream of soldiers coming through the Shoan Gate indicated the entrance of the Shoan army, and shortly afterwards a fanfare of trumpets proclaimed the arrival of their commander. Seated on a gaily caparisoned mule, clothed in rich silks and protected from the sun by a light blue parasol, Dejazmach Balcha entered the market and took formal possession of the town. In the ensuing clean-up many Somalis were slaughtered, but a refreshing tale is told of an old priest who mounted guard over some forty Somali mullahs, stopping the soldiers who came to kill by offering his own life first. To the Somalis he said: 'We are all priests though of a different creed. I will save you to-day; and maybe one day you will save me.'

Under the stern hand of Dejazmach Balcha excitement quickly abated and order was restored.

Meanwhile Lij Yasu, unmolested, made his way with a few followers into the Danakil country.

Thus the overthrow of Lij Yasu was accomplished without bloodshed in the capital, and with general acceptance by the majority of chiefs throughout the country.

It was not to be supposed that Negus Mikhail, Lij Yasu's father, overlord of the warlike Wollo Gallas, himself a man of proved valour and a good soldier, would acquiesce in all this. 'I cannot look on quietly,' he said, and prepared for war. Gathering his forces, he set them in motion early in October against Shoa. The Shoan chiefs found themselves at a grave disadvantage as they were unable to assemble their forces and the forces of those who sided with them so quickly. Some of the big chiefs who under Menelek had been comrades-in-arms with Mikhail and had fought with him against the Italians at Adowa, found it difficult now to decide quickly to make common cause against him. In particular Ras Demissie who was connected with him by marriage; Ras Seyum who was his son-in-law; Ras Walda Giorgis of Gondar; and of course Ras Hailu who, true to type, was sitting on the fence. Ras Tafari had set himself with great address and patience to gain these men over, but he needed time. Ras Lul Seged was sent out with a totally inadequate force to try to hold up Mikhail's advance, but was killed in the bloody battle which ensued, and his troops cut to pieces. Thereupon the Minister of War, Fitaurari Habta Giorghis himself, gathering all the troops by then available, sallied forth to do battle. From Debra Berhan, about eighty miles north-east of Addis Ababa, he sought to save time for reinforcements to come up by opening negotiations with Negus Mikhail. The latter fell into the trap and time, all precious to him, was lost in fruitless parleying. Fitaurari Habta Giorghis even went so far as to send him a gift of ammunition to allay his suspicions.

Fifteen days later Tafari felt himself strong enough to move. Leaving Dejazmach Balcha, who had returned from Harar, to guard the capital, he moved out and the two armies made contact at Sagalle, near Sendafa, only fifty miles from Addis Ababa. The country there is an open rolling plain. The Shoan army was drawn up on the forward slopes of gently rising ground covered in front by marshy land. Ras Tafari himself, taking post with the reserve, directed operations, with Ras Kassa on the right and Fitaurari Habta

Giorghis in the van. Negus Mikhail essayed a night attack but his troops got into difficulties in the swamp, where at dawn they were fiercely attacked by the 'Arada Zabagnoch' (town guards of Addis Ababa) under Aka Gabru supported by the men of Sidamo. There was great slaughter and for a time the day appeared to be going against the Shoans, where-upon Ras Ali, commanding Negus Mikhail's main body, seized the opportunity and launched his men against Ras Kassa's position. The issue hung in the balance until, in the confusion, and in the middle of a furious fight, Ras Ali was taken prisoner. This was the turning point. The Wollo troops gave way and were overwhelmed, and Negus Mikhail himself was captured. The Harar troops, Ras Makonnen's old men, did notable service throughout the battle, and were chiefly instrumental in the capture of Mikhail, who, however, refused to surrender until called upon to do so by Ras Yasaw, who was known to him personally and trusted by him. The Shoans claimed that the prisoners taken by them numbered four to one of their own numbers. Many stories are told of the fight. Ras Kassa was seen at a critical moment to be serving a machine-gun himself. The War Minister, whose position was conspicuous by reason of the green umbrella, the badge of his office, borne beside him, when the umbrella bearer was killed seized and strapped it to his own back, and so continued to rally his men.

The victorious army marched back to Addis Ababa and there was a review on Jan Meda—the racecourse and polo ground. The army, which had camped for the night on the plains below the British Legation, entered from the south end. The review lasted three hours, all the chiefs arriving with their armies and each group having several warriors to rush up to the Empress's tent and vaunt their daring deeds.

The Fitaurari had a great reception, as also did Ras Tafari, who came up with a radiant face.   Then Negus Mikhail was led by on foot escorted by Kagnazmach Imeru.   The survivors of Ras Lul Seged's army, about one hundred, were a sad sight, marching past in absolute silence.   Afterwards his son, wearing just a sheepskin and no head-dress, came, bowed, and sat to one side, where he received the condolences of the other leaders.   Finally came Ras Kassa and the review was over.

6

The Regency

WHAT were the thoughts of this young man as he marched back to the capital after the battle? He was twenty-four years old. For the last ten years, since the death of his father, he had been the maker of his own destiny. Through school, and how insignificant in comparison with modern standards was that schooling; through his first practical experience of administration in a province two hundred miles away from the capital; through the heavier responsibilities of Harar with its more complex problems of government and trade; through the perils and perplexities of civil war, he had stood by himself, with no guide except a strong religious faith, a burning patriotism, and the awareness of his own call to lead.

We are so accustomed to see him to-day as the wise ruler of ripe experience with the tremendous record of adventure and achievement behind him that it is wise to pause and envisage him as he was then on the threshold of his life's work; as he entered on the long fourteen years of regency during which the foundations of a new Ethiopia were laid—and laid by him alone.

We see a young man, slight in build, with handsome intelligent features, the hands of an artist, and an underlying look of steely determination. We find that almost alone among his equals he has been educated, so that he can speak French with fluency, and that he shows an insatiable desire to amass information of all sorts about the outside world. We find that the few foreigners who visit the country are aware of this and appreciate it, and are attracted by a charming and sincere personality that awakens sympathy. But outside his own country he is quite unknown, and inside his own country it is not yet realized that a wholly unique character has stepped on to the stage. All the chiefs recognize that he is a young man of courage, energy, and intelligence; he is invested of course with the prestige of being his father's son, the proclaimed heir to the throne, a representative of the Solomonian dynasty. But they are a little uneasy, all the same. Is he a man of too modern ideas? Will the reforms that he has shown himself already so anxious to introduce mean a break up of the old system, a sweeping away of ancient traditions? Have they done right in entrusting him with the future of their country's welfare— even more important, with the future of their own so jealously guarded positions?

The Ministers appointed by Menelek as an assistance to the ever growing mass of public business had all disappeared from office during the Lij Yasu debacle, but certain personalities of influence were Ras Kassa, Ras Demissie, Ras Abate, Ras W. Giorgis (Gondar), and Dejazmach Balcha. Towering above the rest in influence, however, were the archbishop—Abuna Mattheos, an Egyptian appointed as was always customary by the Patriarch in Egypt—and the old Minister of War, Fitaurari Habta Giorghis. The Fitaurari, as we have seen, showed great valour and took a leading part in the battle of Sagalle. Like our own Wellington after Waterloo he is said to have commented: 'I never doubted we should settle their hash but, by God, it was a damned near thing.' He had risen to his high position under Menelek, who had great confidence in him.

The story is that when Menelek was starting for the front in the Adowa campaign he was short of mules. Habta Giorghis, a merchant in the town, hastily collected his own mules and those of all his friends and brought them to the Emperor. Menelek, greatly pleased, bade him stay by his side during the campaign and was so struck by his capacity and character that he made him his Minister of War when the holder of the title was killed. As time went on and the trend of Tafari's modernizing plans and reforms became apparent, it was natural for these old conservatives to group themselves round the older Empress—the embodiment of conservatism and tradition—and seek through her to obstruct or at best to retard the fulfilment of his various projects. At times the sense of frustration in Tafari was very acute, but in justice to the Abuna and Fitaurari it must be said that they never allowed the political temperature to reach boiling-point. In fact these two older men—the representatives of the religious and secular power—began to assume more and more the role of mediators between the old and the new, though with the scales weighted in favour of the old. Tafari's common sense and an infinite capacity for patience came to his rescue; he realized that so long as the War Minister and the Abuna were alive he could achieve little of an effective nature, and he schooled himself to abide his time, for time was on his side.

But patience was matched in his character by steadiest perseverance; much of the progress he made was more in the realm of his ideas than in what was obvious to the eye. He pondered deeply on the future and what could be done when the time was ripe. The author obtained a sidelight on this in the early twenties. She asked a young Ethiopian who had been in her service and had later obtained employment at the Regent's palace how he liked his new work. 'Oh,' replied the lad, 'I like it very much, and His Highness treats us very kindly, but there is one thing that is a terrible trial. One of us has, of course, to stay up until His Highness goes to bed—and he never goes to bed till the early morning.'

'Why, what is he doing?' 'Oh, nothing. He sits alone in his study, just thinking and thinking and thinking!'

During the years of his Regency the lack of education loomed large in his mind, and he devoted a great deal of his energies to working out a programme and laying the foundations of this vital reform. In 1920 not 1 per cent of the inhabitants, high or low, were literate. Apart from the small school founded by Menelek for the sons of the nobility and a similar school in Harar—the people of Ankober refused one offered to them—there were in effect no schools other than the groups of children who would be gathered round their parish church, and taught the rudiments of reading and writing through the medium of the Scriptures. The Church saw no reason to change this and offered much passive resistance to the infringement of their duties and privileges. Nothing deterred, Tafari greatly increased the scope of the Menelek School and himself founded and equipped the Tafari Makonnen School, which grew quickly to several hundred pupils.

Here are the first words of his speech at the opening of the school on 27th April 1925:

Thanks be to Thee, O Lord our God, infinite and omni-present, that Thou hast led me to finish what by Thy will Thou didst cause me to begin and that Thou hast granted me to speak of this. Of Ethiopia's greatness and antiquity, and especially of the long years when, surrounded by pagans, she struggled for her faith and for her freedom, we ourselves, her own children, can indeed bear witness. . . . But it is not what she was that can profit Ethiopia but what she may become. . . . That knowledge must be sought and found whereby Ethiopia, an African state which has preserved her independence, may be led towards progress and may obtain political stability and the well-being of her people. The task may then be undertaken, but before a task can be undertaken, the tools must be prepared. . . . Education is the tool. . . . Everyone who loves Ethiopia should concern himself with founding schools.[1]

He encouraged his wife, Princess Menan, to found the school for girls which bears her name, and which opened in September 1931. This is a striking tribute to his breadth of mind that he realized, while still so young, the essential need of trained and educated women, and he has ceaselessly striven for the raising of the marriage age for Ethiopian girls.

Into these schools he introduced European teachers, and at the same time began to send abroad—mostly to the United Kingdom and France—a steady trickle of boys who could benefit by a wider education; for the most part these were his own selection and paid for from his own resources. They were to be the tools which he could hope to find ready to his hand when the time came for his schemes of progress to go ahead, unhampered by the reactionary die-hards. How cruelly did fate disappoint him, for many of these young men fell as the victims of Fascist terrorism, and thus there is a gap of a generation still sadly felt in the higher grades of government service.

A few small schools were also started in the provinces at this time, but, whilst the furtherance of education has always been nearest to his heart, improvement in public health has come next. One hospital had already been built in Menelek's time, and staffed by Russian and then by French doctors. To this Ras Tafari added a fine new hospital close to the gate of his own palace, which he named Bethsaida, and at which he was a constant visitor, frequently remaining as an on-looker in the theatre—as he still often does.

Seen in retrospect by far the most important achievement of the Regent was to secure the entry of Ethiopia into the League of Nations. Though he was often thwarted in his

[1] *Speeches of H.I.M. Haile Selassie I*, Part I, 27 April 1925.

efforts at internal reform by the 'old guard,' now definitely ranged in opposition round the Empress, he was trusted in the domain of foreign affairs. His inquiries—and his search for accurate knowledge in every kind of sphere was tireless—led him to believe that in the League of Nations there existed a body that could throw a cloak of protection over the smaller states, and might therefore be a useful aid to Ethiopia against her three powerful neighbours, who had already given evidence that they would not be averse to absorbing Ethiopia into their own territories, or at least into their spheres of influence when the time was ripe.

He was not unaware that an applicant for admission to the League would have certain obligations to fulfil, and when in 1924 the Ethiopian Government submitted its application, it did so happen that Great Britain, Australia, Norway, and Switzerland opposed immediate admission, doubting whether Ethiopia was in fact capable as yet of assuming these obligations. They questioned whether the Central Government of the country was strong enough to control, for instance, the arms traffic, or to suppress slavery.

France and Italy, however, took the line that membership of the League would strengthen the Central Government and in the end Ethiopia was admitted on 28th September 1924, by the unanimous vote of the State members. This was a considerable personal triumph for Ras Tafari, for it was on his growing reputation that the favourable vote was cast. From that day to this, reliance on the League and its successor the United Nations Organization, and steadfast loyalty to its principles have been the keystones of Ras Tafari's foreign policy; and few will deny that he has used with consummate skill its machinery for furthering the interests of his own country. At the same time he realized, and in the matter of slavery took immediate steps to carry out, his country's obligations incurred on her entry to the League.

Even prior to this the Empress, on the recommendation of the Regent, had reaffirmed the edicts published by Menelek against the slave trade, and in March 1924 a law was promulgated providing for the liberation of any slave who could prove cruelty or underfeeding against his master; of all those slaves who had been sponsored at their baptism by their owner, or with their owner's permission had entered the Army or the Church; of any slave whose master had not claimed him within a week of arrest. It was further enacted that slaves who were not liberated on the death of their master (as was frequently done) should serve for seven years only in the household of the heir, after which they should be considered free.

In 1925 it was stated before the League of Nations that cases of slave trading were more numerous in Ethiopia than in all the rest of Africa. The Regent, however, drew attention to the fact that, as the market for slaves still existed, chiefly in Arabia, the states which administered the neighbouring countries where were the ports of embarkation were equally concerned in the traffic; and the Ethiopian Government expressed a desire to come to some agreement with them for combined action. At the same meeting they publicly expressed the intention of obtaining the gradual disappearance of slavery as a recognized institution.

It was as difficult, however, for the Regent to make any immediate change in this direction as it was with most of the other plans which he was so busy conceiving and preparing during the waiting years. It was hoped that better things might eventuate when he became Emperor. Nor were these hopes disappointed.

For over ten years, by steady perseverance, incessant industry, and unflinching resolve, the young man pressed on his way—the way of advancement, as he saw it, for his beloved country. Then in due course the Fitaurari and the

Abuna died in the same year. Tafari began inexorably to force the pace.

One of his first moves was to summon to the capital Dejazmach Balcha, the same man whom we have met earlier as having done good service both for Menelek and at the time of Lij Yasu's overthrow, but who had become one of the most influential among the group of his opponents. He received a summons to the capital, a summons which he chose to disregard. A more peremptory message followed and this time the Dejazmach thought it prudent to obey. He arrived in Addis Ababa, however, or rather on the outskirts of the town, at the head of an army of ten thousand men, and ensconced himself in his own house some eight miles from the heart of the city. This was an obvious challenge to the Regent, who acted with vigour. He invited the Dejazmach to come to a banquet the following day, even acceding to his stipulation that he should arrive with a bodyguard of some six hundred armed retainers. The banquet was held, the conversation was animated, each protagonist seeking to justify his own position. The Dejazmach rode away again unpersuaded. But a surprise and shock awaited him. As he neared his own property he found the compound deserted, his army evaporated into thin air. In his absence the Regent had sent his own men to persuade the provincial soldiers that it was in their own interest to go home without further ado; their immediate interest was satisfied with a present which would see them provided for during the journey—and the advice was followed. Dejazmach Balcha recognized the adroitness of the manœuvre which had outwitted him, and though he sought sanctuary for a few days in a neighbouring church, he was persuaded to give himself up. After retiring to a monastery for some years he presented himself for service again at the time of his country's peril. There is no animosity in the character of the Emperor. Balcha died in October 1936, fighting for his country on the outksirts of Addis Ababa some time after the Italians occupied the capital.

The reactionary party realized that their position was fast becoming untenable, and within two years of these latter events a conspiracy was formed to depose the Regent from his trusted position. It failed, and in September 1928 this failure of the Palace Revolt, as it came to be called, finally established Ras Tafari in his position, and advanced him to the rank of Negus (king). Its story will give an additional picture of his steadiness in danger, and his power of quick decision, if the emergency demand it.

The Regent had gone down, as was his almost daily custom, from his own house—the little ghibbi—to the palace in which state affairs were conducted—the big ghibbi. Hardly had he set foot within the hall when the gates of the palace were closed behind him, and held closed by troops within. Machine-guns, posted on the roof of the Menelek mausoleum, which stands within the wall of the palace enclosure, were trained on the entrances. Within, the Empress was questioning the Regent on rumours reported to her that he was aiming at supreme power. Disposing scornfully of such allegations of disloyalty, Ras Tafari maintained complete self-possession in the face of the threatening soldiers of the palace guard. Ordering the great doors of the ghibbi to be thrown open he passed out and down the steps of the assembly hall. The force of his personality held the crowd. Outside the main gates there had already arrived retainers from his own palace who had been hastily armed with any weapons which his wife, Waizero Menan, who had been apprised of the situation, could lay hands on.

The gates were opened at his orders, his own servants poured in; in the silence of surprise Ras Tafari mounted his

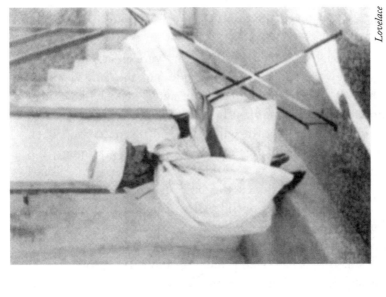

Lovelace

Learning the Amharic alphabet

Lovelace

A priest of the Ethiopian Church reading the
Scriptures

mule and rode slowly towards his own house; his calm
confidence had won the day.

All through this affair eye-witnesses were greatly impressed
by the new vigour and promptitude and the cool decision
with which Tafari had acted. He acted in fact like a man
who knew that his moment had come and was determined to
mould events to his own will. And in the outcome, when
the mutineers were safely under guard and all was quiet, the
Council of State met at the Old Palace, endorsed what Tafari
had done, and petitioned the Empress to raise him to the
status of Negus—thus putting all real power into his hands.
The ceremony which took place a day or two later was
symbolic of this change.

A silken tent had been pitched in the palace grounds over
against the old Church of the Trinity. Here at an early
hour assembled the participants: the Empress Zauditu and
her officers of state, Tafari with his own personal officers,
the Itchegi or chief of the monks, who was acting head of the
Church in the absence of an Abuna. There were present
the *corps diplomatique* and one or two privileged spectators
—the author's husband being one. After some intoning by
the priests Tafari rose and, descending from the throne
erected for him, advanced slowly towards the Empress and
knelt at her feet. Silk hangings were draped around the
pair as the crown was placed upon his head. Then the
hangings fell apart and as Tafari—the king—rose to his feet
there was a startling zip as swords whizzed from their sheaths
and were waved on high. His officers thronging round him
seemed almost to carry him back to his throne. Ensued a
dramatic pause, and then again as though on a sudden impulse
the whole concourse surged round him and bore him off in
triumph to the church hard by, where he was to receive the
acclamation of the people—leaving the Empress alone, a
forlorn figure in the almost deserted tent.

Then when he left the church he drove, wearing his crown, in an open carriage back to his own palace.

The reins of government were now definitely in his hands. One last effort was to be made to snatch them from him. Within a few months of the events just described, a deep-laid conspiracy was unmasked revealing that Ras Gugsa, Governor of Begemder, and former husband of the Empress, was engaged in an attempt to marshal the powerful forces of the north against Shoa and the Regent. He had been forced to separate from the Empress when she was called to the throne, and to retire to the north. For this, and perhaps other reasons, he bore an undying grudge against Tafari; and descended as he was from Ras Wollie of Gondar, he had great influence and prestige throughout the north.

The danger was extreme but Negus Tafari met it with firmness and astuteness. A great battle between north and south was to be avoided at all costs, but Gugsa must be isolated. The Regent's emissaries did their work well, and one by one Gugsa's friends fell away from him. To clinch the business the new Abuna was prevailed upon to excommunicate him. This news and the Church's condemnation of all those who dared to support Gugsa was broadcast in leaflets from an aeroplane—a 'messenger from the sky' not seen before in those parts.

Meanwhile an overwhelming force had been set in motion from Shoa Wollo and Yejjo and was converging on Gugsa. The ensuing battle was brief and could only have one result. Gugsa was killed on the field, and his force, consisting of his personal troops, was overwhelmed.

Meanwhile the Empress, who had been ailing for some months past and who, during the events just described, must have been undergoing severe mental distress, became seriously ill and within a few hours of receiving news of Ras Gugsa's death succumbed. Negus Tafari immediately moved his own personal troops into the palace. His accession as King of Kings was proclaimed and took place smoothly and quietly. The goal had been reached.

Proclamation in the name of the Crown Prince and Regent Plenipotentiary of the Ethiopian Realm, His Majesty King Tafari Makonnen, on his ascending the Imperial Throne with the name of His Majesty Haile Selassie the First, King of the Kings of Ethiopia.

PROCLAMATION

King Tafari Makonnen

In accordance with the Proclamation which our Creator abiding in His people, and electing us, did cause to be made, we have lived without breach of our Covenant as mother and son. Now, in that by the law and commandment of God, none that is human may avoid return to earth, Her Majesty the Empress, after a few days of sickness, has departed this life.

The passing of Her Majesty the Empress is grievous for myself and for the whole of the empire. Since it is the long-standing custom that when a King, the Shepherd of his people, shall die, a King replaces him, I being upon the seat of David to which I was betrothed, will, by God's charity, watch over you. Trader, trade! Farmer, plough! I shall govern you by the law and ordinance that has come, handed down from my fathers.

25 Megebit 1922. (3rd April 1930).

7

King of Kings

RAS TAFARI MAKONNEN succeeded to the throne on 3rd April 1930, and was crowned King of Kings in great state on 2nd November of the same year. 'The Lion of Judah hath prevailed. Haile Selassie I, Elect of God, King of the Kings of Ethiopia.' So ran his title. He took the throne name of Haile Selassie I. This was his baptismal name, which every child receives from the priest at baptism, and which they may or may not use for general purposes.

The position he had already created for himself and his country was evidenced by the fact that many foreign countries sent important representatives to attend the ceremonies. The Duke of Gloucester represented the King of England, the Prince of Savoy the King of Italy, while the French Government sent Marshal Franchet d'Espérey.

Much had been done to prepare the capital city—still in its infancy, in comparison with others—for the visitors. For the first time the two main thoroughfares were faced with tarmac and the old city gates removed. The cathedral of St George was redecorated and a large annexe set up in the garden surrounding it. The police force was put into uniform and in an incredibly short period of training showed themselves well able to maintain order and deal with the enormous increase in street traffic. For in the ten years between 1920, when there could be seen only one car, the property of the Empress, and 1930, when there were hundreds of cars on the roads, the whole aspect of the city streets had changed.

The Emperor and Empress had spent the night in prayer, having gone down to the cathedral the previous evening. Early the following morning the guests assembled and were accommodated in the large tent, where also sat the great Rases who as the Emperor's crown was placed upon his head were to don their coronets. It was a dramatic moment when the Abuna Cyril or Querillos placed the triple crown of Ethiopia upon Haile Selassie's head—a moment also of triumph and fulfilment.

Through the decorated streets and cheering crowds there drove the visionary who had dreamed his dreams indeed, but had used their inspiration to equip himself intellectually and practically for the great task to which he was called, and for which he stood ready.

The midnight cogitations and the experience gained through the regency bore fruit with startling rapidity. The speed and co-ordination of the various steps now taken were evidence that they had been deeply pondered over, and carefully planned in advance.

The first step was the granting of a written constitution, which 'marked the transformation of Ethiopia to a limited monarchy,' even though the limitations of the Emperor's powers were slight. In a speech with which he introduced this great—and entirely voluntary—innovation the Emperor spoke of the moment having come 'to establish a Constitution whereby the whole people may be made to share our labours in accomplishing the heavy task of Government at which former Emperors laboured alone.'[1]

Into this granting of the Constitution was dovetailed the appointments and allocations of duties to ministers, the opening of a Parliament, and the choosing of foreign advisers.

[1] *Speeches of H.I.M. Haile Selassie I*, Part III, 16 July 1931.

In the present age it is necessary that the people of Ethiopia join in the performance of all the work of government; therefore, on this principle, in order that all suitable persons may become participants in the task, we have established two Houses of Parliament. The Members who will consult together in these Chambers will come from various provinces, chosen under the authority of the Emperor, until such time as the people have reached a degree of education and experience enabling them to make the choice themselves. Their decisions will be by a majority vote, and if the Emperor approves them they will be put into effect.

Decisions taken in the Parliament and approved by the Emperor will be executed for the whole of Ethiopia and by the ministers, who will be responsible in the matter and will see that the requirements of government and people are duly fulfilled.

The next step was to reorganize the country's finances, and customs services were overhauled and improved. The Emperor was speaking while on a visit to the custom-house in Addis Ababa:

Nobody can be unaware that in any part of the world whatsoever the vital principle of a government consists in money. As it is the soul that keeps the body alive, so it is money that keeps a government alive through all its difficulties. Well then, a man, whoever he may be, does not cease from the utmost thought and effort to prevent his soul, that is his life, being separated from his body—that is, to prevent his becoming dead—until such time as God has determined for him. And similarly a government, so long as it preserves the name, must exert the utmost thought and activity to prevent the treasury becoming empty of money and difficulties arising over payments.[1]

Then there followed the beginnings of the creation of modern security forces—army and police; accompanied by the organization of 'model' provinces which were to serve

[1] *Speeches of H.I.M. Haile Selassie*, Part I, 22 October 1925.

as experimental and demonstration centres for the reorganization of the whole of the country's internal administration. His own experience joined to his father's teaching
was ready to bear good fruit. A programme for the
improvement of roads and communications was put in hand,
and of course education and health services took a new surge
forward.

In the matter of slavery, reforms proceeded, as had been
hoped. A letter from the Ethiopian representative to the
League of Nations in September 1930 declared that 'sup-
pression of the traffic in slaves is proceeding with thorough-
ness. The Emperor since his accession has notified his firm
resolve to pursue this work rigorously.' The same month
a list of 991 liberations for the year 1929–30 was submitted
to the commission and 399 condemnations in the Slavery
Court.

This 'firm resolve' was borne out by the Emperor's
invitation to the Anti-Slavery and Aborigines Protection
Society to send representatives to discuss the situation and
advise him on it. In 1932 a commission was sent out under
the chairmanship of Lord Noel Buxton. Discussions took
place freely, and if the commission left with a feeling of disappointment that actual accomplishment was slight, the result
of their visit was primarily the promise given by the Emperor
that he would abolish slavery from his dominions within
twenty years.

In all this the inspiration and personal driving force came
from the Emperor. In the absence of trained personnel
and an educated civil service, and the tradition and training
of those around him being what they were, most of the petty
details of administration had to be supervised by him too.
The burden was immense—and how short a time was to be
allotted to him! A bare four years—for by 1934 Haile
Selassie had no illusions as to what the Italians were

preparing—and by that year his mind must be diverted to devising a plan to meet the coming storm.

The granting of the Constitution on 16th July 1931 was Haile Selassie's own idea, and was done of his own volition. This alone would mark him as no ordinary man, for never in history has a sovereign done such a thing on his own initiative. But Haile Selassie, pondering on the past, had come to the conclusion that 'so long as the feudal system continued no real stability or social progress could be looked for.' He was certain that the only way to undermine and neutralize the power of the feudal chiefs was to get the common man on his side, to give him his rights in law, and to govern through parliamentary and democratic institutions. It may be thought that to discover this required no great feat of the brain—but credit is due to the one and only man in the country at that time who was able to take the mental leap over ten centuries.

There was a tendency at the time for observers to doubt whether the Emperor was doing more than indulging in a gesture to impress the world; but he himself lost no opportunity in public or private to make his motives clear. A journalist who wrote an article in 1938 gave his view that Haile Selassie had inaugurated parliamentary institutions more with the idea of giving his people some elementary education in modern forms of government, than with any idea that they should become a reality for many years to come. He showed his article to the Emperor before submitting it for publication and was told, in round terms, that he was wrong; that, on the contrary, the new form of government was designed for the express and practical purpose of breaking down the old feudal system, and that in this task it was already succeeding.

Of the new Constitution here are the salient features. It laid down and defined the powers and prerogatives of the

Emperor, and the duties and rights of the individual. It formulated the creation of parliamentary institutions, the duties of ministers, the administration of justice, and the introduction of a budget system. In the third and fourth articles it stated categorically that the Imperial title was vested in the line of Haile Selassie I, descendant of King Sahle Selassie, 'whose line descends without interruption from the dynasty of Menelek I, son of King Solomon of Jerusalem and of the Queen of Ethiopia known as the Queen of Sheba'; and that the Throne and Crown shall be transmitted to the Emperor's descendants, pursuant to the law of the Imperial House. In accordance with this law and ancient custom the Emperor lost no time in issuing a proclamation designating his eldest son Asfa Wassen heir to the throne.

In selecting his foreign advisers the Emperor was careful not to confine his choice to one nationality. Auberson the legal adviser, was a Swiss; de Virgin, at the Ministry of Foreign Affairs, was a Swede; de Halpert, at the Ministry of the Interior, at first appointed to advise on slavery matters, was an Englishman. Colson, an American, originally appointed adviser on financial affairs, in the end became more and more the Emperor's chief adviser. There were two military missions, one Belgian and one Swedish; and the police were trained by a Frenchman. There were many who prophesied that this mixture would lead to jealousy and lack of co-operation, but in fact these men worked loyally together as a team, and in the troublous times soon to come served the Emperor and the interests of his country with single-minded devotion.

Their work was twofold: to promulgate a policy and to train a staff; while acting as consultants to the Emperor they had as an important part of their duties the task of tactfully instructing and guiding the ministers to whose departments they were attached. It was a work of immense importance and great difficulty, yet the very magnitude of the task, and still more the personality and power to inspire that lay with the man they served, were sufficient incentive to ensure their giving of their best.

The new Constitution—it was the occasion for a banquet and great rejoicing—was signed at the palace on 2nd November 1931, exactly a year after the Emperor's coronation. The dignitaries moved slowly down the hill from the palace to the 'Houses of Parliament'—the new buildings were not yet ready. The great Rases were there, and with all due ceremony took their seats in the Upper House. One or two cameras clicked, democracy was the new order. The system could not of course spring into existence fully fledged; that would have been to create confusion and to court failure, if not disaster. But dawn was breaking over the hills, though in the distance the rumble of thunder could be heard.

'Man may begin an enterprise'—so spoke the Emperor to us, as we stood in the hall of the Menelek Palace—'but it is Almighty God alone who has power to consummate it. We put our trust in God that He will vouchsafe to us that this Constitution which we have established be brought to fulfilment.'[1]

He had need of that trust in the dark days to come.

[1] *Speeches of Haile Selassie I*, Part III, 2 November 1931.

8

War Clouds

'THE tragic episode of international history which is recorded in this volume,' says Arnold Toynbee in his introduction to the second volume of *International Affairs 1935*, 'is a tale of sin and nemesis. . . . If we try to marshal the several participants in the tragedy in their order of merit we shall find that the poorest figure was cut by those with the most specious claim to represent the fine flower of western culture. The "beau role" was played by the Emperor Haile Selassie, the heir of a non-western tradition, who combined an antique virtue with an enlightened modernism.'[1]

How then did the first clouds begin to dim the horizon as the Emperor entered upon the fifth year of his reign?

Ever since 1896, the year of the Italian disaster at Adowa, the Italians had been smarting under their defeat. In 1906 the Tripartite Agreement between England, France, and Italy, though hardly justifiable when looked at through modern eyes, had strengthened the Italian position on the northern boundary of Ethiopia, where a good volume of trade flowed through the Italian colony of Eritrea down to an Italian port at Massowah.

In 1923 Italy had in agreement with France urged the admittance of Ethiopia to the League of Nations. By 1925 the Fascist regime was firmly established and Mussolini well on his upward trend to power. In 1926 notes were exchanged, on British initiative, between Great Britain and Italy, whereby the British agreed to recognize a zone of

---

[1] Arnold Toynbee: *Survey of International Affairs 1935*, vol. ii, p. 1.

economic influence for the Italians in return for an Italian undertaking not to interfere with the waters of the Nile that flow from Ethiopia. The Ethiopian Government—her Emperor keenly alive to the situation—on the publication of these notes in accordance with the open procedure required of all League members, was naturally surprised and indignant, and immediately forwarded notes of protest to the two governments. It was stipulated by the Emperor that these should appear alongside the notes that were published in the 'Treaty Series' of the League of Nations. Then he was silent; his point had been gained. Here was a masterly passivity.

Two years later a twenty years' treaty of friendship was signed with Italy. By this the Regent gained for his country access to the sea by securing a 'free zone' for Ethiopia at the port of Assab, in the coastal strip of Eritrea. A road was planned to link Dessie with this port, both signatories to the treaty undertaking to contribute to its building in their own country, and an Italo-Ethiopian company having the monopoly of the road traffic. This, however, proved nought but a source of disagreement, for the Ethiopians refused to allow Italian engineers within their territory, and the Italians refused to accept the plans proposed by Dutch engineers.

It was petty jealousy and bickering of this kind which fostered the mutual feelings of mistrust and ill will which grew so evident at this time. During the five years between 1930 and 1935, while the Emperor was redoubling his efforts, now that his hands were free, to govern, to educate, to equip, to train, Italy was building up a long series of complaints about frontier raids; though no details of these were ever produced until June 1935, when she complained that Ethiopian irregulars under the leadership of a Somali who was already 'wanted,' were massing near the Somaliland border.

At the same time an attack by the young hot-bloods of Gondar on the Italian Consulate in that town was disavowed by the Ethiopian Government but full reparation was made. However, as late as September 1934 the Italian Government agreed to reaffirm the Treaty of Friendship made six years previously.

The Emperor throughout these harassing and difficult years acted with the greatest patience and propriety. Although he must have seen, step by step, the game which his opponents were playing, he did not falter in his self-imposed tasks of reform and unification within the empire. The Constitution, Parliament, education, justice, finance, as has already been shown, were slowly shaping under his personal supervision and stimulus, against a background that darkened against him day by day.

Yet his faith in the League of Nations, in the protection and friendship of the other great powers, served to buoy him up against the possibility of desertion and disaster. So when the final clash at Wal Wal rang up the curtain on the fearful spectacle of imminent war, it found him confident of the loyalty of his own people, and of the friendship and support of his friends. That confidence, though it stood him finally in good case, was to be tested and stretched to breaking point in the coming years.

The tragic sequence of events which followed the so-called 'settlement' at Gondar is almost too well known to bear repeating.

It was on 6th December 1934 that a peaceful world was startled by the news that fighting had broken out between Ethiopian and Italian troops at a place called Wal Wal in the south-east of Ethiopia, 100 kilometres from the frontier of Italian Somaliland. The Ethiopian troops were the escort of the Anglo-Ethiopian Boundary Commission which had just finished the demarcation of the frontier running with

British Somaliland, and they strongly resented the presence of an Italian garrison sixty miles beyond the frontier of Italian Somaliland. That frontier had never been demarcated on the ground, or even settled in detail; but, according to an old agreement and a recent Italian map, Wal Wal was well within Ethiopia.

There is reason to believe that the tribesmen who joined the Ethiopian troops had been incited by an agent of the Italians to attack their native troops. The Italians used armoured cars and there was heavy loss of life amongst their poorly armed adversaries. The Ethiopian Government proposed that the dispute be submitted to arbitration, but the Italian Government rejected arbitration and demanded heavy compensation. Consequently, the Ethiopian Government reported the incident to the League; and on 3rd January 1935 requested action under Article II of the Covenant. The League Council, however, on 19th January, after having induced the parties to agree to arbitration under the Italo-Ethiopian Treaty of 1928, decided to postpone consideration of the application of the Covenant until its next meeting, ordinarily four months later. Meanwhile it appeared that the parties were not in agreement as to the scope of the arbitration. Italy refused to allow the question of the ownership of the territory in which Wal Wal is situated to be submitted to the Arbitration Commission, whilst the Ethiopian Government naturally insisted that responsibility for the incident could not be assessed without determining which party rightly claimed the territory in question.

By a series of postponements and chicaneries the questions at issue were shelved from month to month. The Commission of Arbitration met for the first time on 25th June, but immediately suspended its sittings as the Italian representatives refused to discuss the frontier question. The League Council, meeting in extraordinary session early in

August, decided that the question of the ownership of Wal Wal was not within the competence of the Arbitration Commission and instructed the members of the commission to meet and appoint an independent chairman.

Meanwhile General de Bono had been sent out to Eritrea at the beginning of the year, and troops soon followed him on the excuse that frontier incidents must be provided against. By March the Ethiopian Government became thoroughly alarmed at the continued flow of troops and munitions of all kinds to Eritrea and Somaliland, and protested to the League again and again from this time on without result. Its efforts to import arms were thwarted by the refusal of the British Government, followed by the French, to issue, from 25th July on, any further licences for the export of arms to Italy and Ethiopia. Italy was not buying in England, but Ethiopia was. Moreover, the French authorities at Djibuti held up consignments of arms for months on the ground that technicalities prescribed by treaty had not been complied with; and when these had been complied with, the railway company after the outbreak of war refused to carry them owing to Italian threats to bomb the railway bridges.

On 3rd September the Arbitration Commission decided that neither side could be held responsible for the Wal Wal incident; but this incident was already almost forgotten in the excitement and apprehension felt throughout the world at the obvious and rapidly growing menace of Italian aggression; for a powerful army well supplied with transport was already lined up on the Eritrean frontier, the Italian air force in the colonies had been multiplied many times, and several new aerodromes had been laid out.

Britain and France had indeed made proposals thought likely to be advantageous to Italy for modernizing the administration of Ethiopia and opening the country to economic development and exploitation by foreigners, in a conference at Paris in the middle of August; but these proposals were summarily rejected by Signor Mussolini, and he refused to formulate alternative terms to his demand for a protectorate over the whole country.

On 4th September the League Council at last began to take the threat of war seriously, and appointed a committee of five to examine the situation and propose a settlement. In the Assembly of the League on 11th September Viscount Templewood (then Sir Samuel Hoare) made his famous speech, which contained the following noteworthy and reassuring passages:

The ideas enshrined in the Covenant, and in particular the aspiration to establish the rule of law in international affairs, have appealed . . . with growing force to the strain of idealism which has its place in our national character, and they have become a part of our national conscience. . . . The League stands, and my country stands with it, for the collective maintenance of the Covenant in its entirety, and particularly for steady and collective resistance to all acts of unprovoked aggression. The attitude of the British nation in the last few weeks has clearly demonstrated the fact that this is no variable and unreliable sentiment, but a principle of international conduct to which they and their Government hold with firm, enduring, and universal persistence.[1]

Yet there was also a qualification, the importance of which was not generally realized until some three months later, as follows:

If the burden is to be borne, it must be borne collectively. If risks for peace are to be run, they must be run by all. The security of the many cannot be ensured solely by the efforts of a few, however powerful they may be.

Actually, as Professor Arnold Toynbee has observed:

[1] Arnold Toynbee: *Survey of International Affairs 1935*, vol. ii, p. 187.

Lovelace

The harbour at Massowah

Tony Boyadjian

One of the castles at Gondar

It was not the public proceedings in the Assembly, but a previous conversation between Sir Samuel Hoare and M. Laval on 10th September, which determined the League's action and sealed Ethiopia's fate; for these statesmen, representing the two leading nations of the League, privately agreed on that day that no action should be taken under Article 16 in the nature of sanctions of a military character or of a kind which would involve any risk of war with Italy. [1]

The committee of five failed to produce any kind of plan which would satisfy both parties and, in view of the attitude adopted by Italy, there seemed to be nothing further that could be done in the way of conciliation. The Assembly adopted a watchful attitude, and decided to remain in session after the normal business of the annual meeting was concluded.

This was the position when Italian troops crossed the Eritrean frontier on 3rd October 1935, and began their advance upon Adowa, under the command of General de Bono. Simultaneously General Graziani opened hostilities on the frontier between Ethiopia and Italian Somaliland.

Meanwhile, faced with a situation which rapidly deteriorated throughout the year, the Emperor, though he delayed until the last possible moment, had done his best to prepare for the inevitable. But what were his chances? It is true that the frontiers of the Ethiopian Empire, and the central plateau of the Amhara people, formed one of the great mountain fortresses of the world, but were these natural advantages sufficient to counteract the advantages bestowed on Italy by her complete command of the weapons of modern war; weapons which were denied by the western powers to Ethiopia?

The order for general mobilization was not issued until 29th September 1935. This was the Emperor's own decision

[1] Op. cit., pp. 188 and 192.

in the face of much criticism. Although in the previous
six months thousands of Italian soldiers had passed through
the Suez Canal on their way to Eritrea—and Ethiopia—it
was used by the Italian High Command as the pretext for
marching into Ethiopia.

So the drums sounded at the big gate of the old Menelek
Palace that opens on to a wonderful view of the city and its
surrounding mountains, and as the excited crowds scrambled
up the rocky hill to hear the news, there was read out the
proclamation of mobilization, informing the people that the
Italian army had on Wednesday, 2nd October 1935, crossed
the Mareb and begun the invasion.

9

Aggression and Occupation

THE Italian campaign was entrusted to Marshal de Bono in the north and to General Graziani in the south. Eventually, their two armies met and joined hands in the capital.

The invaders made good use of modern methods of warfare. For years Italian agents, usually in the form of consuls or medical missions, had been instructed to spread the idea that Italian assistance would be forthcoming to such non-Amharic peoples as were wishful to shake off their allegiance to the Shoan Emperor, as they called him. If by these fifth-column methods Ethiopia could be absorbed into Italian colonial possessions—well and good. If not, other and sterner weapons must be sought to assist Italian expansion.

Assembled in Eritrea were thousands of vehicles, vans, tanks, and lorries which had been passing through the Suez Canal for the previous six months. In them were massed cylinders of poison gas, suitable for spraying on man and beast, should they prove intractable. Massed on the new-made airports were 300 aeroplanes—bombers and fighters which were to combat the half-dozen of the Emperor's air force.

It remained to be seen whether the loyalty of the component parts of his empire would stand proof against such intrigues; whether the valour of the Emperor himself and the troops he led would stand fast in the face of this new 'terror of war; whether the natural defence of mountain and valley, rift and canyon would deny passage to the invader.'

It is certain that the first weapon played a large part in the opening of the campaign in the north where Italian influence had been at work for many years, playing upon the jealousy of the northern provinces who had originally owned the dynasty and the capital, which had now been surrendered to the newly established Shoan hegemony. The entry of the Italians into the northern section of Tigre was greatly facilitated by the defection of Dejazmach Haile Selassie Guksa, son of Guksa Araia, who had been deprived of the governorship of Tigre in 1932. He was a descendant of the Emperor John, and it had been to bind him more closely to the throne that the Emperor had given him his second daughter, the Princess Zenab Worq, in marriage. But she had died in 1934, and he was resentful at the loss of a considerable part of his patrimony at his father's death.

As soon also as it became evident that the Emperor's army was retreating before the enemy, the Azebo and Wollo Gallas, tribes in the east of the escarpment, hastened to pay off old scores, and severely harassed the retiring troops.

As a result of this the Italian armies, once across the frontier, found the occupation of Tigre, and its capital Adowa, an easy task—and the capture of this last with its bitter memories of defeat was the occasion for great jubilation. Ras Seyum withdrew before them after a fruitless defence of his province and the Italians immediately issued proclamations as to their peaceful intentions, if the population would accept their terms. They claimed a bloodless occupation of the country that had originally belonged to them.

Meanwhile, in the south, General Graziani under more arduous conditions of heat and desert country, and hampered by rain, was making slower progress tòwards his objective of Harar province and town, and the railway beyond them. His plan was that of intensive air bombardment—a new and terrible experience for the Ethiopian troops in that bare and open country—and then advance to take advantage of panic and despair among the armies.

The first three months of the war, however, still gave some hope that the enemy might be held or delayed until the advent of the rains in the second half of the year might hamper his advance. This proved a vain hope. The Italians brought into use the second of their weapons. In 1936 Marshal de Bono, as a result of his refusal to use poison gas to speed up the invasion, was superseded by Marshal Badoglio, and the latter now began to press southwards. He had utilized the delay imposed on him at Makalle to build up his army, construct his roads, and organize the forces and ammunition at his disposal.

The first blow to the Ethiopian defence in the north was the defeat in the Tembien of the forces under the command of Ras Kassa and Ras Seyum; though they had made a gallant stand for some months without any major disaster, they were finally forced out of the region. Meanwhile, Ras Mulugeta, the Minister of War, and a veteran from the days and the fighting of Menelek's campaigns, had established himself at Amba Aradam, a strong defensive position. On 10th February a battle was fought here against Italian troops advancing in two columns. This resulted in a severe defeat for the old Ethiopian general, who was surprised by an intrepid assault by Alpini troops from an unexpected quarter which he had thought inaccessible; he was able, however, to withdraw his troops, or what was left of them, in good order to the main road, though he himself died from pneumonia as a result of over-fatigue and exposure.

The Emperor, who had earlier paid a visit to the southern sector of the war, had now returned to Addis Ababa, and proceeded north to Dessie, which he made his headquarters and where he assumed command. To the north-west Ras

Imeru and Dejach Ayelle were gradually forced out of the area north of Lake Tsana and the Italians had occupied Gondar and Gallabat on the Sudan frontier. After the defeat of Ras Mulugeta at Amba Aradam the Emperor pushed north from Dessie towards Lake Ashangi where the main Ethiopian army had retreated, in the hope of rallying his forces; and here he took command in the field. It was during this period that intensive use was made of mustard gas, which was dropped in containers and sprayed from the wings of aeroplanes on combatants and non-combatants alike—even upon the undergrowth that might afford them cover. Against this the Ethiopian soldiers were entirely without defence.

Meanwhile from his position near Kworam the Emperor was threatened by the two Italian columns who were advancing from the north and north-west; and now there was a further threat from the east, where a column from Assab was reported to be advancing, and to have already entered Sardo, the capital of the Aussa Sultanate. This was a serious danger, for this place was only one hundred miles from Dessie. Though attack from here would mean an arduous march through the heat of the desert, and a climb up the steep escarpment on the edge of which Dessie stands, the establishment of an air base would constitute a grave threat to the rear of the Emperor's army.

It was in these circumstances that the Emperor struck first. Never perhaps has his personal courage been more clearly demonstrated than in this frontal attack against an enemy already flushed with easy victory—an enemy infinitely better armed, organized, and equipped. He had decided perhaps that he must either fight or make good his retreat without delay; his generals were men of the old school who knew no other methods of warfare than massed attack, and who were scornful of guerrilla tactics and confident of their ability to fight. However that may be, this decisive action of the war was opened on Ethiopian initiative, and in it the Emperor himself took an active part, firing a machine-gun for two days without sleep.

Although at first successful, fighting gallantly against withering fire from machine-guns and standing on their own against heavy artillery fire, in this final battle at Mai Chaw, north of Lake Ashangi, the Ethiopian army, under the personal leadership of the Emperor, was finally defeated. After four days of hard fighting it was routed and fled in disorder. Down the road to Dessie poured the troops, harassed by intensive air bombardment as well as by attacks from hostile and rebellious tribes of Azebo and Wollo Gallas along the road.

Marshal Badoglio followed up his victory with determination and speed, and within ten days his troops had entered Dessie. The Crown Prince, just twenty years old, remained there until the enemy were almost in sight, but unable to put up any defence against intensive air bombardment retreated towards Addis Ababa. As the survivors from the northern front straggled back into the capital their condition and the gloomy reports they brought of the situation gave rise to general despondency. Yet the Emperor himself gave no such indication. On 19th April an order was issued by the Government calling upon the whole male population capable of bearing arms to report for military service. On 30th April the Emperor, together with Ras Kassa and some others, returned to the town, and it was reported that the Government was planning to retire westwards, and reorganize resistance from some other headquarters. His return journey had been arduous and dispiriting through the mountainous country west of the main Dessie–Addis Ababa road. On more than one occasion treachery and brigandage among rebellious local tribes had revealed to him how much intrigue and propaganda had been at work within his own country—and he had had more than one narrow escape.

Yet on the evening of 30th April he told foreign correspondents in the capital that he intended to fight to the end. But a further blow awaited him; he learned of the defeat of his army under Dejazmach Nasibu in the south, and when he issued an appeal on 1st May for every able-bodied man to march northward to repel the invader, there was practically no response.

This disappointment, coupled with the possibility that perhaps the Galla people in the west would prove hostile to the idea of the war penetrating to their country, and with the almost intolerable strain, physical and mental, to which he had been subjected, caused the Emperor to change his mind. He had already arranged for the Empress and members of his family to leave the country, and at the last moment he decided to accompany them down the railway line. He would himself carry the case of his country to the Tribunal of the League. The possibility of defence from Dire Dawa had occurred to him, but as he passed through he heard that advanced Italian troops were already in his home town of Harar—thirty miles away. With his family, Ras Kassa, his Foreign Minister, Belatingeta Herowi, and a few other followers, he passed on to Djibuti, where he was met by a British warship which conveyed him and his family to Haifa.

With the departure of the Emperor the seat of Government was removed to Gore and the following account of the situation was issued on 8th May in a letter to *The Times* from the Ethiopian Minister in London:

A group of Ministers are still carrying on the Government in the west and are in possession of the archives which were saved from Addis Ababa. . . . Under present conditions it would not be politic for me to reveal the position of the

Government headquarters, as this would merely invite the use of bombs and poison gas in the area.[1]

On 9th May Mussolini announced to the Italian people the passage of a decree annexing Abyssinia to Italy, and investing the King of Italy with the title of Emperor of Ethiopia. Marshal Badoglio was on 10th May appointed Governor-General of Ethiopia with the title of Viceroy and with full powers.

[1] Arnold Toynbee: *Survey of International Affairs 1935*, vol. ii, p. 357.

10

Exile

THE Emperor left Dire Dawa by train for Djibuti on 2nd May and on 3rd May he embarked in a British cruiser which took him, his immediate family, and his much trusted Foreign Minister, Belatingeta Herowi, to Haifa, where he landed, to proceed immediately to Jerusalem. On the roof of the Church of the Holy Sepulchre is an Ethiopian scene in miniature: priests of the Ethiopian church reside there, in tiny houses, replicas of the country huts of their homeland.

Here he spent a fortnight—resting physically after the rigours of the campaign which had tried him hard, gathering courage and energy spiritually for the conflict that he still must wage. An acquaintance whom I met in London that same summer, and who was a true friend of the country and its ruler, expressed with some vehemence how much better it would have been, in her view, had he died at the head of his army, fighting valiantly—but in vain. But was it not the realization that he had a sacred duty still left to him as the temporal and spiritual head of his afflicted country, a duty which only he could perform, that decided him to come in person to the League—to fight not against guns and gas in the hills and valleys of his native land but against 'spiritual wickedness in high places' in an international arena, carrying out those responsibilities which he had already shouldered 'for the whole of Humanity'?

Again he travelled on a British cruiser, which took him safely through the Mediterranean and landed him this time

in England, where he was received with acclamation by a
large crowd gathered in London. There was deep seated in
the British people a feeling of impotent discontent at the
whole sorry tale of injustice, that could find an outlet only in
this way. Certain it was that wherever he went he made
friends and won respect and admiration. This was not just
sentimentality for the leader of a lost cause, but an expression
of sympathy and understanding, an awareness of the principles
of right, truth, and justice for which this Christian ruler of an
African state was fighting—single-handed. On 10th May
the Emperor had sent a telegram from Jerusalem to the
League of Nations Secretariat in Geneva:

We now demand that the League of Nations should continue
its efforts in order to ensure respect for the Covenant, and that
it should decide not to recognize territorial extensions, or the
exercise of an assumed sovereignty, resulting from an illegal
recourse to armed force and from numerous other violations
of international agreements.[1]

Immediately he set to work energetically to receive reports
from Geneva, and prepare himself with the help of his Swiss
and American advisers to present in person his final appeal to
the League.

On 27th June a note was addressed to the States members
of the League by Dejazmach Nasibu on behalf of the Emperor.
In it he stressed the incompleteness of the Italian conquest;
the existence in the unoccupied part of the country of a
government with which the Emperor was in communication,
and on which he had conferred full powers; the insistence of
the Emperor on his full rights and his continued demand that
States members should fulfil their obligations under the
Covenant.

Two days later Haile Selassie appeared in person to address
the Assembly. Undeterred by the exhibition of hooliganism

[1] Arnold Toynbee: *Survey of International Affairs 1935*, vol. ii, p. 483.

by Italian journalists, who had to be forcibly removed, he
rose to speak—a small slight figure 'with the triple claim to
consideration conferred on him by his personality, his rank,
and his fate.'[1]   There can have been no scene in the whole
history of the League Assembly more profoundly moving
than on this tragic occasion—no speech more justified in its
reproach, no prophecy more pregnant with doom.   In it is
his clear expression of his deep sincerity, of his unalterable
and unshakable faith in the righteousness of his cause, of his
sureness of the final triumph of good over evil.

I, Haile Selassie I, Emperor of Ethiopia, am here to-day to
claim that justice that is due to my people and the assistance
promised to it eight months ago by fifty-two nations who asserted
that an act of aggression had been committed in violation of
international treaties.   None other than the Emperor can address
the appeal of the Ethiopian people to these fifty-two nations.

There is perhaps no precedent for the head of a state himself
speaking in this Assembly.   But there is certainly no precedent for a people being the victim of such wrongs, and being
threatened with abandonment to its aggressor.

.   .   .   .   .

In order to kill off systematically all living creatures, in order
the more surely to poison waters and pastures, the Italian
Command made its aircraft pass over and over again.   This was
its chief method of warfare.   The very refinement of barbarism
consisted in carrying devastation and terror into the most
densely populated parts of the territory—the points farthest
removed from the scene of hostilities.   The object was to
scatter horror and death over a great part of the Ethiopian
territory.

These fearful tactics succeeded.   Men and animals succumbed.
The deadly rain that fell from the aircraft made all those whom
it touched fly, shrieking with pain.   All who drank the poisoned
water or ate the infected food succumbed too, in dreadful

[1] Ibid., p. 490.

suffering. In tens of thousands the victims of the Italian mustard gas died. It was to denounce to the Civilized World the tortures inflicted upon the Ethiopian people that I resolved to come to Geneva.

.   .   .   .   .

The Italian provocation was obvious. I did not hesitate to appeal to the League of Nations. . . . Unhappily for Ethiopia this was the time when a certain Government considered that the European situation made it imperative at any price to obtain the friendship of Italy. The price paid was the abandonment of Ethiopian independence to the greed of the Italian Government. This secret agreement, contrary to the obligations of the Covenant, has exerted a great influence over the course of events.

.   .   .   .   .

It was constantly repeated that there was not merely a conflict between the Italian Government and Ethiopia, but also a conflict between the Italian Government and the League of Nations. That is why I refused all proposals to my personal advantage made to me by the Italian Government if only I would betray my people and the Covenant of the League of Nations. I was defending the cause of all small peoples who are threatened with aggression. What have become of the promises that were made to me? . . .

I assert that the issue before the Assembly to-day is a much wider one [than that of the situation created by Italy's aggression]. It is not merely the question of a settlement in the matter of the Italian aggression. It is a question of collective security; of the very existence of the League; of the trust placed by states in international treaties; of the value of promises made to small states that their integrity and their independence shall be respected and assured. It is a choice between the principle of the equality of states and the imposition upon small Powers of the bonds of vassalage. In a word, it is international morality that is at stake. . . .

No subtle reasoning can change the nature of the problem or shift the grounds of the discussion. It is in all sincerity that I submit these considerations to the Assembly. At a time when my people is threatened with extermination, when the support of the League may avert the final blow, I may be allowed to speak with complete frankness, without reticence, in all directness, such as is demanded by the rule of equality between all states members of the League. Apart from the Kingdom of God, there is not on this earth any nation that is higher than the other. If a strong Government finds that it can, with impunity, destroy a weak people, then the hour has struck for that weak people. I appeal to the League of Nations to give its judgment in all freedom. God and History will remember your judgment. . . .

What prophetic relevance in view of the events of the next three years. Mr de Valera in commenting the next day upon the speech said: 'Does any delegate deny that, in so far as it relates to what has happened, there is truth in every word of it?'

His appeal made, his warnings uttered, the Emperor returned to England, where he found a house on the outskirts of Bath, and retired into private life. This did not mean any cessation of his determination to maintain to the best of his ability his country's rights as a member of the League of Nations, and to this end he devoted himself for the next eighteen months.

During the summer the lifting of sanctions against Italy was yet another disappointment to the friends of Ethiopia. The defeat and surrender of the two generals, Ras Desta, son-in-law of the Emperor, who was foully murdered as a prisoner; and of Ras Imeru in the west, put an end to any immediate hopes of organized resistance.

A new and more pressing problem arose by September of the same year. Although Haile Selassie was still recognized as sovereign by all countries except Italy and Germany, questions were asked at the September Annual Session of the League Assembly as to the credentials of the Ethiopian delegation. Could these be considered valid, issued as they were by the Emperor of a state which he no longer actively administered? The question was after much discussion referred to the International Court of Justice at the Hague. Meanwhile the delegation took its seats as before.

This point temporarily shelved, the position was safe-guarded; but still further disappointments made bitter the year that followed. One by one the member states, headed by Italy and Germany, and closely followed by Austria, Hungary, and Switzerland, recognized Italian suzerainty over Ethiopia. This rendered still more difficult the status of Ethiopia for the following annual meeting in September 1937, and the Emperor, after taking the advice of well-known legal experts, decided that it would be unwise to put the question of credentials to the test. He therefore suggested to the Secretary-General that as Ethiopia had no business to put before the Assembly, he would postpone the appointment of a delegation. If the permanent delegate at Geneva were to inform him that any matter relevant to the position or status of Ethiopia had arisen, he would immediately appoint a delegation to take its seat in the Assembly. For this purpose three persons remained in Geneva in case of emergency; credentials signed and sealed were there ready to present should need occur. They did not have to make use of them. Ethiopia could not be expelled from membership of the League, save for misdemeanour in violating its provisions; this could certainly not be laid to her charge.

So a wise passivity in the face of defeat, discouragement, and disappointment ruled the Emperor's policy at Geneva. Meanwhile he himself, watching, waiting, working to safe-guard all that he could of his country's interests and to keep alive in man's memory the very fact of her existence, set to work to gain knowledge of men and affairs, and to impress his personality upon all with whom he came in contact.

His quiet dignity in public, his unaffected and winning cordiality in private life won him many devoted friends. Though puzzled and disheartened in his relations with the British Government at this time—and still more so when in July 1938 it became evident that they and many others were preparing to recognize the *status quo* in Ethiopia, and acknowledge the Italian annexation; yet he always could feel that there was good understanding and sympathy between himself and the man in the street. There was no doubt that the British public as a whole felt keen sympathy for him, they considered that he had right on his side and had been given a raw deal. By a curious chance the author's husband was a witness of an instance of this feeling. He was sitting in a carriage at Paddington station. An express was alongside his train, about to leave for the west, and in the express, without his knowing it, was the Emperor on his way down to Bath. The whistle blew for the express; suddenly the door of his carriage was flung open and a big bluff grey-headed guard precipitated himself into the compartment, scrambled through into the corridor beyond, threw down a window, and leaned out towards the moving express with every evidence of excitement. Obviously a crisis was imminent in the working of the Great Western line. But no! A minute later the guard relaxed, pulled up the sash, and came back through the compartment looking very much pleased with himself. Then no doubt feeling that an explanation was called for remarked with great fervour: 'That's the man for me!' 'Who? What? What are you talking about?' 'Oh! it was Haile Selassie sitting in that train. You know, the Emperor of Abyssinia!'

Of his life in Bath there is little that is not known to the British public. At his house, Fairfield, he led a quiet and unassuming life, sometimes walking down into the town, where he made many friends and performed many kindnesses.

A small chapel was fitted up in the grounds. That side of his character—his complete faith in the ultimate triumph of right, in the sure protection of Almighty God—was abundantly evident in his speech and his actions, and supported him through many dark and difficult days.

Here his trusted Foreign Minister, Belatingeta Herowi, died, to the great grief of his Imperial master, who felt deeply this severance of a link with the days that had been. But younger men were ready to take up the work, and in the darkening clouds of European politics there shone a gleam of light.

The Munich crisis of 1938 had its repercussions on the Ethiopian situation. There were many who saw in it the inevitability of conflict—conflict in which the western democracies must unite to combat the ideologies, gone mad, of Hitler and Mussolini; conflict in which Ethiopia might be in a key position on the way to the East.

Many reports were coming in from Ethiopia, of unrest, of growing resentment, of Ras Ababa Aregai with his many thousands of followers holding out in the district between the road and the Danakil desert. Letters would arrive confirming loyalty, describing local revolts against Italian rule, asking for arms, appealing again to the Emperor to speak to the League on their behalf.

News arrived of the existence of a group of young educated Ethiopians, who had formed a committee of 'Union and Collaboration' to pass news and organize guerrilla warfare in the occupied areas. Ras Ababa Aregai and Dejazmach Gherassu Duké were both writing long letters to the Emperor boasting of their active independence of Italian domination— telling of their raids and the numbers of their followers. Ras Ababa claimed to have an army of 10,000 men near Ankober, ready to head resistance to Italian misrule. There was a printed news sheet issued and circulated by these young men throughout the empire. In order to link up these activities, and obtain accurate information, the Emperor dispatched a trusted official, Ato Lorenzo Taezaz, to make his way into the country via Khartoum and report to him on the situation.

Thus hope grew as more and more evidence reached him that the fires of revolt were smouldering ready to burst into flame when the moment came.

Lorenzo Taezaz, after several months spent in Gojjam, where he travelled openly, wearing an officer's uniform, returned with a valuable report which he communicated to Middle East Headquarters in Cairo as he passed through. By the winter of 1939 he was back in England with news to gladden and inspire. The author, with whom he stayed for a few days after his return, well remembers the glowing confidence with which he spoke of the situation as she drove him up the snowy roads to speak with Lord Lugard—ever a faithful friend to Ethiopia—and establish contacts that would touch off the fuse at zero hour. It arrived on 10th June 1940, when Mussolini stabbed France in the back and declared war against Britain, using his troops in Ethiopia to invade the Anglo-Egyptian Sudan and British Somaliland.

Never did he commit a more foolhardy act. Within a month the Emperor, despite difficulties and delays, was in Khartoum, and the flames that finally consumed the Italian Empire in East Africa were being energetically fanned into a blaze by a small group of British and Ethiopian comrades in arms known as Mission 101.

The wheel had come full circle, and the Emperor was with his own again. The tardy allies had arrived.

The Return

ON 10th June 1940, the same day as Italy declared war, letters signed by General William Platt, commanding the troops in the Sudan, had crossed the frontier on their way to Ethiopian chiefs in Gojjam, Armachaho, Wolkait, and Begemder. These letters were in the following terms:

Peace be unto you. England and Italy are now at war. We have decided to help you in every way possible to destroy the common enemy. If you are in need of rifles, ammunition, food, or clothing, send as many men and animals as you can spare to the place which our messenger will tell you. We can help you with your requirements. Also it would be a good plan to send your personal representative to consult with us and to arrange the best means of attacking the common enemy.

During the preceding six months careful plans had been made for the dispatch of Mission 101, consisting of five English and five Ethiopian officers, with money and letters of credence, to penetrate the circle of fortresses that surrounded Gojjam and to contact the leaders, to give news of the outside world and to stir up enthusiasm amongst the patriots who were still holding out against Italian rule. The head of the Mission was Colonel Sandford, and the Emperor's representative was Azazh Kabada, later to become Governor of the city of Addis Ababa and later still Afa Negus or Lord Chief Justice. Their task was to blaze the way for the Emperor's return, seeing to it that the fires that they kindled should spread disaffection and revolt against the Italians throughout the north. They carried with them the Proclamation from the Emperor making known his arrival and calling upon the people to rally to him.

For security reasons warning of the Emperor's impending arrival had not been given to the Governor-General, Sir Stewart Symes, or General Platt, and when on 26th June a signal was received saying that he would be in Wadi Halfa the next day they were somewhat startled, to say the least of it, to have this new and heavy responsibility so suddenly thrust upon them. From the military point of view they were on the defensive. Though the outbreak of war had been the opportunity for the R.A.F. to bomb Italian aerodromes and fuel tanks and for armoured patrols from Kassala to take the offensive in raids on the frontier, by 4th July the enemy had replied in force and, though the garrisons managed to extricate themselves with little loss, Kassala and Gallabat were occupied by the Italians. That no suitable accommodation was available for his unexpected guest and that very special measures for his safety would have to be taken did not perhaps loom so large in General Platt's mind as the fact that he himself placed little value on operations carried out by other than the regular forces under his own command. Symes for his part still clung to the forlorn hope that he could keep his Sudanese out of the world conflict. They both felt that they were being hustled into carrying out a policy which they did not approve, and for which they were not prepared.

Sandford, who had been up in the Gallabat area studying his plans for getting his mission into Ethiopia, returned to Khartoum in the early morning of 28th July. He was instructed to fly forthwith down to Wadi Halfa to discuss with the Emperor his immediate plans. At the same time he was to inform him how meagre were the resources available for any forward movement into Ethiopia. As may be imagined, the Emperor, who had left London believing that plans were well advanced for him to cross the frontier at the head of an army of liberation, was bitterly disappointed and greatly upset.

It was arranged that he should continue his journey to Khartoum as soon as arrangements for his reception were in order, and he duly arrived there on 3rd July, and was accommodated in a villa on the banks of the Nile to the east of the town. Extraordinary precautions were taken to preserve his incognito for the first few days until security arrangements had been tested and found to be adequate. To meet him in Khartoum were brought the leading Ethiopians who had been living in exile in Palestine, including Ras Kassa and the Itchegi, the Head of the Monasteries. His younger son Prince Makonnen had come with him.

Meanwhile the messengers, who had left with their letters on 10th June, were bringing back the answers; and as chiefs with their soldiers came down to the frontier in response to the invitation to collect arms and ammunition, they were brought to Khartoum and presented to the Emperor to give him the latest news and to plan co-operation.

It had been intended that Mission 101 should cross the frontier as soon as possible after the Italians came into the war. The Emperor, however, feeling that, as things were, it might be many months before his original idea of riding in at the head of his army might materialize, now suggested that he himself should accompany the mission. This for many reasons was impracticable, but the discussions caused delay in the start of the mission. A further hold-up was caused by the necessity to await the arrival from Palestine of Azazh Kabada, who had been chosen to accompany Sandford as the Emperor's personal representative. This was an excellent choice that added enormously to the authority and usefulness of the mission. It was not until 12th August that Sandford and his party slipped across the frontier road at dusk, and were lost to view in the tall grass and scrub for the next three weeks.

Meanwhile the Emperor sat in Khartoum, waiting, working out projects for his own return, and chafing at the delay. It was a slow and discouraging business.

There was, however, progress in some directions. A general invitation had been broadcast to all Ethiopians who wanted to fight for their country to assemble in Khartoum. These began to arrive in considerable numbers, and were accommodated in a suitable camp at Soba, where part of the Ethiopians who had been mustered in East Africa were also brought. The training of these men was undertaken by British officers, and a training school was opened also for young Ethiopian officers. A considerable number of arms were issued to patriots just across the border; and then at the end of August a large caravan of pack animals arrived from Dejazmach Mangesha Jambari, one of the most important leaders in Gojjam, escorted by 200 men under the command of Shalaka Mesfin, an officer well known to the Emperor. This party had had a brush with the enemy before they succeeded in slipping through. To welcome and inspect them the Emperor was flown to Gedaref, and great was the propaganda value of this, for when these men got back to Gojjam with their arms, 'Janhoy is here!' they said. 'We have seen him with our own eyes!'

On 27th September the Feast of the Cross was celebrated in the traditional manner by the Emperor and his suite and all the Ethiopians assembled in Khartoum.

At the beginning of September messages began to come in from Sandford by runner and over the wireless, which brought cheering news. He reported that he had been able to establish his headquarters at Sakala in the heart of the mountains in western Gojjam, close to the source of the Blue

Nile; that he and Azazh Kabada had secured co-operation amongst the leading Gojjam chiefs—in particular Dejach Nagash and Dejach Mangesha Jambari; and that the advent of the Emperor was eagerly awaited. He told of operations undertaken by the patriots which were causing sufficient alarm to the Italian High Command to make them send reinforcements from Addis Ababa. He was able to report that the sight of British aeroplanes, and above all the dropping of ammunition and supplies at his headquarters, had caused an enormous sensation. In November he was able to report that Ras Hailu had been sent back to Gojjam by the Italians in the hope that his influence might—from the Italian point of view—restore morale and stop the defection and desertions of local chiefs and *banda*. The Italians were at this time making great use of propaganda, chiefly in the form of leaflets dropped from planes, but most of it was quite ineffective. There was, however, one particularly clever effort in this line. A leaflet was dropped purporting to be the copy of a proclamation by the Emperor appointing Dejazmach Mangesha Jambari Governor of the whole of Gojjam—an appointment which would have made him overlord over all the chiefs of the rival faction, the members of Ras Hailu's family, and would have split Gojjam in two and destroyed at one swoop all the peace-making and healing of old feuds that Sandford and Kabada had so laboriously achieved in the past three months. Within a few hours horsemen began to arrive in Sandford's camp with messages from the mission's most useful supporters showing their extreme perturbation. The situation was indeed unpleasant and Azazh Kabada and his staff showed great uneasiness. The proclamation had all the outward marks of being genuine. It bore the Emperor's seal; the writing, so they said, resembled that of one of the Emperor's secretaries; and at the top there was a reproduction of a photograph of the Emperor landing from a British aeroplane at Gedaref. But really the whole thing was too clever to be true. Proclamations are formal documents drawn up in traditional form. The photograph looked out of place and there was an extra official seal on the top of the document which was unusual; and finally it was incredible that the Emperor should have been so maladroit. The matter was soon settled. The wireless was working; a question was asked and answered: the proclamation was a forgery and the horsemen were soon speeding back to allay the alarm, and the incident ended in a good laugh!

The long period of inaction in Khartoum, however, came to an end early in November. Mr Churchill had for some time been discontented with what he considered to be the lack of initiative shown in the conduct of affairs in Africa. Especially was he incensed with the fact that no use was being made of troops available in East and South Africa.

On 28th October Mr Anthony Eden arrived in Cairo, where he met General Wavell, discussed the situation with him, and then flew on to Khartoum to stir things up. The result was immediate. Plans which had long been simmering but never reaching boiling-point were put into immediate operation.

General Platt was given reinforcements from the Middle East, but for a strictly limited period. He was to invade and overrun Eritrea and then sweep down into Ethiopia from the north. General Cunningham with troops available in East and South Africa should march into Ethiopia from the south; and Haile Selassie with such forces as could be collected for the purpose was to strike in at the centre and exploit the favourable situation that had by now been created in Gojjam by the activities of Mission 101.

Now for the first time the breezes of action began to allay the fever of anxiety and impatience in the house on the Nile. Few people knew who lived there. Now he could talk with someone who had the will and the authority to get things

done. He asked that all available refugees in the Sudan
and Kenya, including Eritrean prisoners of war, should be
assembled, drafted into his bodyguard and other formations,
and their training should begin at once. All this was agreed
to and set in motion. Major Orde Wingate, who was later
to acquire such fame in guerrilla warfare, and who was at that
time in Cairo, was appointed to General Platt's staff. An
energetic and capable artillery officer, he had made his name
in Palestine, where he espoused with great fervour the Jewish
cause. For the next six months his job would be to organize
and equip such forces as could be collected and to put them
at the Emperor's disposal. On 20th November Wingate
flew into Gojjam to confer with Sandford and inform him of
what was toward.

Within ten weeks from Eden's arrival in Khartoum all was
ready and the forward move began. Further, a heartening
message from Sandford seemed to offer good augury for the
future. On 17th December into all the bustle and turmoil of
preparation word came from him that although the local
situation seemed critical he was convinced that the boldest
measures could be taken and might end in the campaign being
over before the rains.

On 19th January Platt's army crossed the frontier at
Kassala; the Emperor marched in at Um Idla on the Sudanese
border with Ethiopia the next day. General Cunningham
launched his first attack in the south on 24th January.

The Emperor's crossing the frontier at Um Idla was the
occasion for a short ceremony at which the flag (safely stowed
away during the occupation) was raised, and by the publication of a proclamation to all his people—I quote below.

A new era has arrived when all will be able to serve their
beloved Ethiopia in their different spheres with greater zeal and
surer strength.

Gracious God who has turned His merciful face does so on

each one of us. Therefore we now forgive those of you who
have worked against the interest of your Emperor and your
country, whether you worked from force, or from your own free
choice: under Italian control, or whether you worked from
outside Italian control.

At the same time he issued this appeal:

I reason with you to receive with love and to care for those
Italians who fall into the hands of Ethiopian warriors, whether
they come armed or unarmed. Do not mete to them according
to the wrongs which they have committed against our people.
Show that you are soldiers of honour with human hearts.
Especially do I ask you to guard and respect the lives of children,
women, and the aged.

The Emperor's little army—or escort—at this stage consisted of the 2nd Ethiopian Battalion, raised from among
refugees abroad, a battalion of the Sudan Defence Force, and
his own bodyguard—a total of perhaps two thousand men.
The plan was to concentrate this small force at Belaia, a great
mountain mass rising out of the plain half-way between the
frontier and the Gojjam escarpment. To service and provision this force fifteen thousand camels strung out along the
hard and relentless road through the broken country around
Belaia. Repeated attempts by motor transport to break
through the bush had failed. Once the Emperor's own lorry
rolled over, and repeatedly he himself got out with his lords
and officers to build stone tracks over the almost impassable
country. All along the track lay the bodies of the camels
dead and dying. The Emperor counted fifty-seven of them
one day; pointing to one: 'He too has died for Ethiopia,'
he said.

It was the Sudan Defence Force who reached Belaia first
under their commander, Colonel Boustead, going by the way
of the old caravan route. The Emperor with his bodyguard
went in farther north over country only half reconnoitred

and trackless—marching on a compass bearing. Wingate's motive had been to screen the Emperor's march, as far as possible, from the Italian garrison at Gubba, only fifty miles away. It proved a tiresome precaution, for the march took fourteen days instead of four or five, and the trucks conveying the Emperor and his suite had finally to be abandoned; a weary company arrived at Balaia on 6th February.

His faithful body servant, Asfaw—later to become a Fitaurari—arrived a few hours earlier to see that the arrangements for the reception of his royal master were suitably in order. Sandford was intrigued to notice an inquiring glance pass between the Emperor and his old servitor as he entered the shelter prepared for him and found all in order. Later he found out that Wingate, who was desperately short of riding animals in the emergency created by the failure of the vehicles to get through, had in ruthless and peremptory tones refused a mount to Asfaw, and prevented him from securing one. History does not relate what wings Asfaw acquired to enable him to arrive before time and have all comfortable for his master. But he certainly did not have the appearance of one who had arrived on foot!

The presence of the Emperor at Belaia acted as a magnet. From all sides men began to pour down to greet him. In a shelter that had been prepared for him, chiefs and retainers came, to prostrate themselves, to tell in the *fouqara* of their brave deeds, and how many Italians they had killed. It was well that there was much coming and going, stories to listen to, and plans to make, for the long wait on this isolated hillside must have been hard to tolerate. So near, and yet so many miles to go. Stores, ammunition, supplies of all kinds for a six months' campaign had now to be transported up the track before the first move could be made. The Emperor had arrived in Belaia on 6th February. On 21st February Wingate and Boustead who commanded the Sudan

Frontier Battalion began their forward march with Burye in Gojjam as their objective.

Sandford, his work in raising Gojjam against the invader finished, had come down to Belaia to take up his new work as principal Political and Military Adviser to the Emperor. There was no transport and he had to walk down the sixty miles in a pair of sandshoes, all that was left after six months of journeyings hither and thither among the mountains of Gojjam.

He had assured Wingate and Boustead that they would be able to press up the escarpment without opposition, as indeed proved true; and once up on the plateau level they pushed on quickly, through Ingebara to the small town of Burye, leaving behind them a trail of peasants along the road to repeat in excited whispers 'He himself is here.' Torelli, the Italian commander, had evacuated Dangila and withdrawn his force of more than one thousand men to the town of Bahardar Giorghis, where he was invested by a company of Sudanese for nearly two months. Then the Italians evacuated Burye, and a message was hastily sent back for the Emperor to come in as quickly as he could. A trail had been blazed up the escarpment and the Emperor left in a truck driven by a French Canadian, le Blanc. Safely negotiating the hastily constructed mountain track he entered Burye in triumph; the *feu de joie* let off by the patriots that night was far more dangerous than any shots fired in its defence by the enemy.

Burye now became the Emperor's headquarters, and while Wingate with his diminutive force of little more than six hundred men hung on the trail of the retreating enemy, ten to fifteen times their number, the 'build up' for the next move was prepared. Stores slowly accumulated by air and by road; air communication was established with Khartoum, and before long his two sons joined the Emperor by this means. 'Operational centres' were briefed here for their respective jobs, furnished with mule transport, and sent off to do them. This meant that a young British officer, together with three or four British sergeants and a hundred or so Ethiopian soldiers who had been given some training in the Sudan, and had been issued with modern rifles and such mortars and light machine-guns as could be spared, would be sent off to stiffen the better organized of the patriot forces, and give them greater effectiveness in clearing the Italians from various outposts all over the country.

The first of these centres was pushed up to join Wingate, who was in the hills north of Debra Markos doing his best with the resources available to him to give the Italians there no peace. When the Keren battle was at a critical stage General Platt requested that everything possible should be done to prevent Italian reinforcements reaching the battle. The Emperor had already dispatched Ras Biru northwards to Debra Tabor, and two operational centres were immediately sent to join him. Their operations round Debra Tabor materially assisted in pinning down the Italian troops in that area.

Meanwhile the Emperor spent long hours every day receiving the Gojjam chiefs, and other patriot leaders from farther afield. It was essential as the troops moved forward to leave some form of stable administration behind them, and to find stable elements in Gojjam, where cohesion had never been the strong point, was not easy. It was essential too that on this return journey after the five years abroad no offence should be given, no sense of grievance aroused. He must also show his appreciation of the patriot effort in the traditional manner. This entailed arranging opportunities for each leader to parade before him, when he and his men could make their *fouqara*.

The situation of the Italians in Gojjam was now becoming

precarious. Keren had fallen to General Platt and his army on 27th March. Cunningham's troops were already advancing from the south. Under this force of circumstances the Italians withdrew from Debra Markos, crossed the Blue Nile on 3rd–4th April; the town fell to Colonel Boustead and his small force, and the Emperor moved in to take possession of the town and to receive the submission of Ras Hailu, and to be welcomed by the many thousands of countrymen who swarmed in to see their Emperor.

On 6th April General Cunningham's forces entered Addis Ababa, and on 10th April Brigadier Lush, the deputy chief political officer and Sandford's brother-in-law, flew from Addis Ababa to confer with the Emperor and Sandford at Debra Markos. Sandford flew back with him the same day, bearing with him the Emperor's views on the forthcoming operations. It was now that patriot activities took on a larger aspect. General Cunningham, after receiving the surrender of Addis Ababa, had sent his troops in the main towards Jimma, in which direction the major part of the Addis Ababa garrison had withdrawn, but the course of events in the north made it imperative that his troops should take part, with General Platt's from the north, in rounding up the enemy's main army, which seemed likely to make its stand on the Amba Alagi massif, the decisive battleground of three previous campaigns. It was necessary, therefore, that the patriot army should help to occupy the attention of the very considerable forces of the enemy in the south-west while Cunningham thinned out his troops in that area in order to provide men for his thrust northwards. It was also necessary that patriot forces should assist in this thrust also.

The Emperor provided forces in four different areas: first on the great north road, to assist the northern thrust; secondly, on the roads leading from the capital to Jimma; thirdly, on the Lekemti road west of the capital, to hold up any diversion that might be made by General Gazzera, commanding the Italian troops in Wallega; and fourthly, to round up the Gojjam garrison, which had retreated by the main roads into the difficult country north-west of Addis Ababa. The Emperor's preliminary instructions were given to the various leaders while he was still in Gojjam. Ras Ababa Aregai, the great patriot leader who had kept resistance against the Italians simmering ever since the fall of Addis Ababa in 1936, was instructed to send five hundred men immediately to co-operate with the South African forces attacking Dessie, and these men were dispatched by lorry within twenty-four hours of receiving the order and did most useful work during the attack on Dessie. The leadership of the patriot forces converging on Jimma was given to Gherassu Duké, another fighting soldier who had never surrendered to the Italians. Shalaka Mesfin and Azazh Kabada (Sandford's colleague in Gojjam) commanded the patriots against Lekempti. To Ras Kassa the Emperor assigned the work of rounding up the Gojjam garrison, in conjunction with such of Wingate's force as could be spared. Wingate himself, as was fitting, commanded the final assault, and thus had the satisfaction of finishing off in person the job he had begun four months earlier.

The last march into Addis Ababa must have been a moving and a heart-warming experience. Driving in from the gorge of the Blue Nile at the head of a long string of cars, past the wreckage of Italian vehicles that lay strewn along the road in mute evidence of hasty retreat, the Emperor would have seen from some fifty miles away the line of the Entotto hills that stand sentinel round the city. Rising to a height of some 10,000 feet they entirely obscure any trace of the capital city that lies to the south of them. The road winds across the long plain of Salulta, keeping close to the foot-hills to avoid the floods of the rainy season. There was a halt at

Fiche to make arrangements for the Emperor's entry into
Addis Ababa; a pause at the ancient monastery at Debra
Libanos, to remember with grief the treacherous shooting of
Ras Kassa's two sons and the execution of two hundred
monks who had been charged with concealing rifles and
sheltering patriots; then the approach to the foot-hills and
finally the climb up the last 2,000 feet to the church of St
Mary that crowns the summit. Here was a delegation of
senior British officers sent by General Cunningham to receive
the Emperor. But first of all into the church went the
Emperor and his sons to give thanks to God for the mercies
vouchsafed to them. As he came out the view of his capital
burst upon him. The procession was formed; and down the
steep road, eucalyptus fringed, came the liberators, Wingate
on his white horse at the head of the 2nd Ethiopian Battalion
leading the procession; the Emperor and his lords; the
Englishmen who had worked with and for him; and last, but
not least, the smiling faces of the Sudanese of the Frontier
Battalion who had helped in the long trek to victory. Lining
the road were the patriots under their indomitable leader
Ras Ababa Aregai, who had watched and fought and waited
for him through the long five years.

'On this day,' said the Emperor as he stood on the rostrum
in the old Menelek palace, where Lt-Gen. Sir Alan Cunningham, G.O.C. East Africa Force, and a guard of honour of the
King's African Rifles had met him,

which men of earth and angels of Heaven could neither have
foreseen nor known, I owe thanks unutterable by the mouth of
man to the Loving God who has enabled me to be present among
you. To-day, I must first tell you, is the beginning of a new era
in the history of Ethiopia. In this new era new work for all of
us begins.

Let us go briefly over the history of those evil days through
which Ethiopia has had to pass. When Italy committed her

H.I.M. the Emperor Haile Selassie in his study

first aggression on our independence which we had maintained for thousands of years, our warriors won the victory of Adowa and saved our independence. The origins of that campaign are not only to be found in the clauses of the Treaty of Uccialli. Italy believed that the moment had arrived for her to crown her old unceasing intrigues and to rule Ethiopia. After her defeat she pretended to be Ethiopia's friend, but she secretly prepared another aggression which, delayed by the Great War, came into the open in the last few years.

Though Italy when she invaded our country was clearly our superior in modern arms, it was our duty to defend our country to the best of our ability. When she used poison gas against our people and defeated them, we were compelled to go to the League of Nations to appeal for justice. This aggression that Italy had begun was sure to spread through the entire world. Responsible statesmen in the world did their best to bring peace to the world and to prevent the fire from spreading. Great Britain, our greatest friend, received us at this time separated in the spirit from the people of our country whose blood was cruelly shed by the Italians; from the churches and those who suffered in the mountains and wildernesses of their own.

During those years how many young men and women, priests and monks, were cruelly murdered by the Italians! In Yekatit, in the Year of Grace 1929, on the feast of St Mikhail [17th February 1937], you know that thousands of people were massacred. The blood of those has cried aloud, whose bodies were split with spades and shovels, axes and hammers, who were stabbed to death with bayonets and stoned and killed with clubs, who were burned alive with their children in their houses and died of hunger and thirst in the prisons! Everybody among you knows that this cruelty was practised not only in Addis Ababa but in almost every corner of Ethiopia. No single person has not suffered, been trampled down and humiliated.

Five years ago exactly to this day the Fascist military entered our capital. Mussolini then announced to the world that he had established a Roman Empire in Ethiopia. The nations who recognized his conquest of Ethiopia believed that he would hold the country for ever. The martial qualities of the Ethiopian are universally known, but we had been unable to import the arms necessary for our defence because we had no seaport. Mussolini had been pronounced the aggressor by fifty-two nations, but that was nothing to him; he boasted the more! So the past five years were an age of night for you, my people, but you grazed like sheep upon the mountains of Ethiopia and you did not surrender your hope! In those five years your patriots [*arbegnoch*] endured all hardships and maintained your liberty, and the Italians did not dare approach the mountains where you grazed.

Though the enemy did not control the country, yet he spent many thousands of millions of lire to exploit that part which was under his control. This money was not spent to raise the standard of living of the oppressed Ethiopians nor to compensate them for Italian aggression; but to establish a Fascist colony and a brutal rule in our sacred land. The enemy did not offer Ethiopia a mandate or a protectorate, which in themselves are a harsh yoke upon the independence of a nation; all that he wanted was the annihilation of the races of Ethiopia.

But the end of the thousands of millions of lire spent here was not what Mussolini thought that it would be.

When Italy declared war in order to snatch the booty of conquered France she had a mass of men, guns, and money in Ethiopia. Her troops numbered not less than 150,000 and she had foodstuffs for many years. She thought that she was so prepared as to be impregnable. But what has happened is not in accordance with Fascist aspirations. The *spirit* and *morale* that are so important a weapon in modern war were revealed in you. Because you co-operated and knew the enemy's methods, because you understood one another and were the warriors of *one nation*, you were able to defeat an enemy superior to you in arms and men.

The English were fighting on many other fronts for the liberation of the world, and they needed time to prepare the liberation of Ethiopia. You patriots meanwhile obliged the enemy to remain hidden in his fortifications, you cut his communications and made his life a burden to him. He had powerful defences; but you taught him that his tenure was short and that he could not long remain among people who disliked him and his ways of government. He learned that the people around him were stronger than he, and he abandoned the hope of meeting his other strong opponent with his remaining forces.

When the time came that our ally the Government of Great Britain was ready to attack the enemy in full force, I came with my soldiers from the far Sudan on our western boundary, and entered the heart of Gojjam. The enemy in Gojjam had powerful forts and a powerful army, aircraft, and guns. He was twenty times as strong as us in every respect. Besides this, we had no aircraft or guns at our command when we needed them. But my presence alone among my brave people gathered thousands of men, and the enemy's panic was ever increasing. While my troops were cutting his communications and pursuing him beyond the Blue Nile in Shoa and Begemder, I heard the happy news that the formidable armies of Great Britain had occupied our capital and were pushing northward to Dessie and southward to Jimma. The army of the Sudan had smashed the enemy's strong positions at Keren.

I therefore gathered my men who were scattered everywhere in pursuit of the enemy, and I am in my capital to-day. My happiness is boundless: I have been granted the opportunity to lead my own soldiers, crush our common enemy, and reach Addis Ababa. I owe thanks without limit to Almighty God, who has enabled me to be with you to-day in my Royal Palace from which the Fascist Government has been forced to flee!

People of my country Ethiopia!

On this day Ethiopia indeed stretches out her hands to God, shouting and telling out her joy to her own sons!

This day also is the day when Ethiopia will yearly celebrate her national feast, for it is the day of the liberation of the sons of Ethiopia from the heavy yoke and the chains of the stranger's government, and the day when we are reunited with our dear and loving people, severed from us for five years. On this day we will remember the heroes who loved their country and gave themselves for her, who shed their blood and crushed their bones to defend that independence which they had inherited from their ancestors, who honoured their King and their Flag.

Those sufferings which we have sustained in the last five years and of which we forbear to speak shall be a lesson to us. It is for you to aid us in the work of progress which we will undertake on behalf of Ethiopia. You shall be united, honouring and loving one another. In the new Ethiopia we want you to be an indivisible people, equal before the law, free men all.

You are to collaborate with us in our endeavours to develop the country, to enrich the people, to increase agriculture, commerce, and education throughout the land, to protect the life and wealth of the nation, and to complete those changes in our administration necessary to our new condition.

Since to-day is a day of happiness for us all, for on this day we defeated the enemy; therefore you should rejoice heartily in the spirit of Christ. Do not reward evil for evil. Do not commit any act of cruelty like those which the enemy committed against us up to this present time. Do not allow the enemy any occasion to foul the good name of Ethiopia. We shall take his weapons from the enemy and make him return by the way that he came. St George who slew the dragon is the patron both of us and of our allies. We should therefore fasten our friendship for ever in an indissoluble bond, to defeat this ungodly and newly spawned dragon that vexes mankind. Our allies are our friends and our own blood. Take them to your hearts!

Back in his own palace a mile away which had been made ready for him, the Emperor stood with a small group of personal staff and British officers. 'Vraiment, j'ai été très emotionné,' he said.

12

Putting the House in Order

'YOU are to collaborate with us in our endeavours to develop the country, to enrich the people, to increase agriculture, commerce, and education throughout the land, to protect the life and wealth of the nation, and to complete those changes in administration necessary to our new condition.' There must have been many who gasped at the calm assumptions involved!

The Emperor stood at the top of the double flight of steps that lead to the great reception hall of Menelek's old palace. He had pulled up the Ethiopian flag as below him there stood the guard of honour of British troops provided by General Cunningham who had been at the gates of the palace to welcome him. In the open spaces between the hall and the gateway—that same gateway from which had been read the proclamation of war against the Italian aggressor—stood the people, the priests of Addis Ababa churches, the men and women who had waited, suffered, and hoped for this day. The sun shone fitfully, the rain clouds gathered behind the eastern rim of the Entotto hills. The Italian population of Addis Ababa—25,000 in all—had all been bidden to keep within their doors. It was, as the Emperor said, a day 'which neither men nor angels could have foreseen or known.'

In this era of cataclysmic changes memories tend to become short; and it is hard to recall how formidable was the task to which the Emperor now committed himself and his people, when he returned to his country and took up the reins of government. There was no part of the country which had not been visited by war in the six months preceding his entry, and many districts had been ravaged over and over again during the previous six years. Shattered buildings, broken bridges, and abandoned transport met the eye wherever one went. The country was full of rifles, machine-guns, and bombs captured from and flung away by the fleeing enemy. Just about a year later a friend of mine found a hand grenade in the drawer of her kitchen table. 'Where did this come from?' she asked the cook, with some asperity. 'Oh, I found it lying about,' said he, 'and it's useful to throw at the "jibs" [hyenas] when I go home at night.' And a bullet fell through my roof one night in 1942.

These weapons were by no means all in the hands of house-boys or peaceful peasantry, desiring nothing better than to get back to their homes at night or to their ploughing by day. They were largely in the hands of disbanded soldiers of the Italian native army, or of patriot guerrillas, who after years of outlawry required time and opportunity to become once more members of a peaceful community. These unruly, or at best unsettled, elements of the population had to live, or were in fact living 'on the country.' The Italian administrative machinery had, of course, disappeared. Means of communication had been dislocated, and the roads were dangerous in more ways than one. Trade was dead, and in many districts there was a shortage of the necessaries of life —of salt, clothing, and, in some large areas, even of food.

The progress made in the first few months in bringing some sort of order out of this chaos was astonishing and reassuring. In general the whole country remained quiet, and there were few districts to which normal life had not returned. Roads, with some exceptions, were safe; the country markets were thronged. The roads and tracks leading to the capital again resounded to the shouts of the muleteers bringing in their loads of hides and skins, coffee, wax, and grain. Driving up from Nairobi about a year later I was warned that it was not safe to go ahead of the military convoy of vehicles as we climbed the steep escarpment below Mega—but my car would not keep to the chugging pace of the lorries, so we went on and drew up to wait at the top. An oldish man came along the road and, interested in my car load, stopped. 'Four children!' he said. 'Why, you 'll want some milk for them,' and he handed me an old Menelek silver coin; 'get it for them in the next village.' We sat down to lunch to drink it outside the ruined Italian fort that crowned the hill.

Within a short time governors and judges had been appointed to all provinces and districts. The distribution of these posts had been far from a simple matter, many of the old and well-tried men had disappeared in the turmoil of the past five years and it had not been easy to find others to replace them. Neither rank nor merit could be the sole password to office. There were patriot leaders to be justly rewarded for past services, and the fighting soldier is not necessarily the best administrator.

Obviously this did not all come about with the waving of a wand. Pending the time when the Emperor could get all the threads back into his own hands, some rough and ready machinery had to be devised for preserving law and order and maintaining essential services. The problem was complicated by the presence in the country of an Italian civil population numbering 40,000, who had to be evacuated, but in the meantime protected, housed, fed, and medically cared for. All these services had to be organized at top speed. There was no means of supplies reaching Ethiopia from Djibuti, the roads to and from Nairobi and Berbera were rough; lorries were short.

The machinery introduced for these services was the

Occupied Enemy Territory Administration—a singularly ill-chosen name in the case of Ethiopia—which was controlled by the political branch of the military command headquarters at Nairobi. That these heavy responsibilities were successfully shouldered—and they included such tasks as organizing staging camps for the Italians and their families on the way to the coast, the upkeep of roads and railways, the maintenance of light and water services, such as they were, in the bigger towns, and the organization of transport for bringing in supplies—was a feather in the cap of an efficient and very hard-worked staff.

The British military authorities did not always perhaps fully appreciate the magnitude and extreme urgency of the problems facing the Emperor. The soldiers had, in truth, little time to consider them. They were concerned, to the exclusion of everything else, with winning the war against the Axis. Having, by the elimination of the Italian forces in Eritrea and Ethiopia, removed a threat to their rear, their first duty was to rush the troops northwards again, to meet the assault that was being mounted against them in the Western Desert. When the fall of Gondar in November 1941 released the British troops employed in that operation, Haile Selassie asked that they might be employed temporarily in disarming the Raia and Azebu Gallas, disaffected and warlike tribes, inhabiting the low country in the east of Tigre province. They had been armed by the Italians for the special purpose of causing trouble along the main line of communications between Eritrea and Addis Ababa. He was told by the British commander that no troops could possibly be spared for this, as they were behindhand in the time-table for moving northwards. This was no doubt true, but the rapid and complete withdrawal of all British troops before his own forces of law and order could be adequately organized was to create a dangerous situation for the Emperor.

Haile Selassie, of course, from the moment General Cunningham's troops reached Addis Ababa, realized only too well what the tasks before him were, and was in a fever to get full control into his own hands, so that, as master in his own house, he could deal with them. A perhaps absurd illustration of the differing points of view may be given. In the early days after his return, certain of the legal advisers of O.E.T.A., far from wishing to expedite his gaining control, were worried about the legal aspect of his position.

'His Majesty Haile Selassie I,' they said, 'cannot fully reassume his status and powers as Emperor until a peace treaty with Eritrea has been signed with Italy.

'Until that happens' (and of course everybody knew that a peace treaty was a matter for the dim and distant future) 'the King of Italy must remain the legal ruler of Ethiopia!'

In any case the difficulties inherent in any system of dual control made it imperative not to prolong the life of the British administration for longer than necessary. For dual control it was from the start. It was of course to the Emperor, from the moment he entered his capital, that the people looked to for orders and for justice, and not to any foreigner, friend, benefactor, or comrade-in-arms though he might be. It was a matter of satisfaction, therefore, to all parties when the Anglo-Ethiopian Agreement, which provided for the full re-establishment of the Ethiopian Government, was signed at Addis Ababa on 31st January 1942.

This agreement was a working arrangement, providing for collaboration and mutual assistance between two allies, during the period that must elapse before world peace could be restored. It was subjected to a good deal of ill-informed criticism, as was also the military convention that accompanied it. It was forgotten that these agreements were never intended to have more than temporary force to tide over a phase of restoring order out of disorder, and that it was impossible at that stage to be precise about the shape of things to come. The two governments wisely confined themselves to making practical arrangements for the near future, with regard to the fact that the war outside Ethiopia was still raging. Within the next few months came the fall of Singapore, the retreat of the British Army from Libya, and the fall of Tobruk. The immediate objects in view were to safeguard Allied military interests, pending the final expulsion of the enemy from the remainder of Africa; to ensure the safe removal from Ethiopia of all Italian prisoners of war, and of all but a small proportion of the Italian civil population; to provide a judicial system which could be satisfactorily applied to both Ethiopians and foreigners; and to supply the Emperor with such assistance, financial and otherwise, as to enable him to re-establish his administration. That all these objects were achieved so quickly that the agreements outwore their usefulness before the minimum period (two years) of their currency had elapsed, was proof that the confidence of the British Government in Haile Selassie had not been misplaced.

It should not be forgotten that when the agreement and military convention were signed, Djibuti was still held for the Vichy Government and was under blockade by the Allied forces; the critical days of the invasion of Egypt by Rommel were yet to come. It was reasonable that while these conditions prevailed the vital allied communications which passed through the Ethiopian Empire should be secured by British troops, and that special powers and responsibilities should be vested in the Allied Commander in Chief in certain areas. Happily for all, Africa was soon purged and freed, so the conditions which necessitated these arrangements disappeared.

It was in 1944 that the Emperor made his trip to Suez to meet President Roosevelt, who had flown over to Cairo to confer with Winston Churchill, and it was at this meeting that the President issued the invitation to visit the United States, which was later implemented by President Eisenhower, and resulted in the state visit of 1954. But it is clear evidence of the settled state of the country that within three years of his return the Emperor should be able to leave with a quiet mind in order to pay this complimentary visit.

Though the restoration of law and order was the main task during the first three years, an immense amount of general constructive work was carried through at the same time. A glance at the Statute Book will tell the tale. Between 30th March 1942, when the *Negarit Gazeta*—as the official gazette is called—was first established, and 30th December 1944, seventy-one proclamations or laws were promulgated. These covered such differing subjects as the administration of justice and the composition of the law-courts and their rules of procedure; the organization of the police force and the administration of prisons—a pressing and most essential piece of legislation; the powers and duties of ministers and administrative regulations for the provinces; public health, the control of dangerous drugs, and the registration of medical practitioners; the control of enemy aliens and the custody of enemy property—there was plenty of it lying about all over the country; the establishment of a State Bank and the regulation of currency and legal tender; the establishment of a land tax and of personal and business taxes and export duties. One of the laws concerned the abolition of the legal status of slavery—the fulfilment of a promise made by Haile Selassie to the Anti-Slavery Society some twenty years before.

By the end of 1944 the Emperor's administration was

firmly established. In spite of gloomy prognostications from a few pessimists it had only once been seriously challenged— by malcontents in Tigre province in the autumn of 1943. When we reflect on the size of the empire, the diversity of the elements of which it is composed, and the state of chaos in which the Emperor found it on his return, we can pay tribute not only to the skill, sympathy, and patience with which he carried out his task, but safely affirm that he suc- ceeded because his people believed in him, trusted him, and wished him—and no one else—to succeed.

The short-term phase of reconstruction was now over. Law and order were restored, the government once more functioned adequately. This state of affairs was signalized by the signature, on 19th December 1944, of a new agreement with the United Kingdom, placing the relations of the two governments on an equal footing without any special privi- leges being accorded to the British Government, except in one respect. The Ethiopian Government agreed—not very willingly—that the territory known as the Ogaden, which borders on French and British Somaliland and the former Italian colony of Somalia, and which is inhabited by nomadic Somali tribes, should remain under British military adminis- tration for the time being. It is questionable whether there was adequate justification for British insistence on this pro- vision. Their relinquishment of it in the agreement recently entered into has certainly removed a cause of resent- ment.

All these and many other pressing problems were dealt with in these busy years—and to have accomplished this in the face of the dissolution of the old semi-feudal system which preceded the Italian war, and the demoralization and anarchy prevailing during the Italian occupation, is a tribute that should be duly paid to the Emperor and those who advised and assisted him. The actual physical labour—his hours of work are from early morning to late at night—must have been terrific; but also the mental effort involved to re-create a state from its elementary beginnings and raise it to the dignity of a world recognized polity, would alone place Haile Selassie among the great men of our time.

13

The Next Ten Years

1. The Economic Background

AS recorded in the preceding chapter, the business of 'putting the house in order' was by the end of 1944 sufficiently completed for the Emperor and his ministers to begin to take longer views regarding the development of the empire and its peoples. The programme they began to envisage, though never announced in the modern manner as a five-year or ten-year plan, covered almost every form of governmental activity. It had as its main features the creation of modern security forces, well appointed and well disciplined army and police forces; the improvement of roads and communications of all sorts; and the expansion of educational and health services.

Obviously none of this could be achieved unless financial resources could be found without upsetting the economic balance of the country. The success in realizing this aim is perhaps the most striking achievement to date of Haile Selassie's administration.

No doubt Ethiopia has during these ten years been greatly blessed in that she—alone among the countries surrounding her—has enjoyed peace and tranquillity. Little doubt also that she has been very fortunate in that the soaring world price of coffee—her largest export—has generously greased the wheels of the state coach. But, all this would not have availed unless the economic structure had been well designed and well built.

It is not within the scope of this book to attempt a technical appreciation of the economic policies of the Ethiopian Government of which the Emperor is the head, its aim is to record the aims and achievements of the Emperor. But as the programme we are discussing was in its general aspects the dream of Haile Selassie since early days, and as its fulfilment, as we have said above, depended and will continue to depend on its financial background, we cannot avoid touching briefly on these matters.

The first budget to be passed by the Ethiopian Government was published in the Appropriation Proclamation of 1944. It estimated the revenue for the year 1945 as Eth. $38,200,000, or roughly £5,440,000.

Ethiopia being an agricultural country with few industries, there could not be much flexibility in the revenue, and it certainly could not find the surplus required for an ambitious programme of development. What could be the solution? A good deal could be done by fiscal reform—by providing efficient central control of all taxation—and by introducing new taxes that would not bear on land and agriculture. The most significant of these were the steady and drastic scaling up of customs duties on imports, and the introduction of a personal and business tax in 1943. Much also could be done by improving the financial mechanism of trade.

Currency and exchange were subjected to controls as soon as possible, and these have amply justified themselves. The situation as regards currency when the Emperor first returned was fantastic. A traveller proceeding from the north to the south in the lowlands near Dessie stopped to purchase a few oranges, proffered a pound note to the young Adal Somali who was offering them and demanded change. Without turning a hair the youth produced from the pocket of his sole garment, a khaki shirt, a bulging wallet containing Egyptian piastres, East African shillings, rupees from Aden, francs, and lire, and suggested that the traveller should help himself. Neither party to the transaction had any very clear ideas as to who had gained by it.

In the old days the sole legal tender had been the Maria Theresa silver dollar. These coins were stamped with the head of the Austrian Empress of the eighteenth century; though they were not introduced into Ethiopia till 1850 they had been circulated in Iraq and Arabia for a century. By the beginning of the twentieth century, so deeply rooted was the detail of the design in the minds of the Ethiopian country folk that they would examine and reject any coin that differed in the smallest respect—even the number of pearls on the Empress's veil, or the size and twist of the lion's tail. When Menelek issued dollars impressed with his own effigy they refused to take them into general use; so it is still the old dollar with the head of the Austrian queen of two hundred years ago that is the only widely known metal currency.

The new Ethiopian currency—notes of $1, 5, 10, 50, and 100—is the sole legal tender. It is based on the United States dollar, and is a very sound proposition; its legal backing is laid down as 30 per cent but at the moment of writing stands at 40 per cent. Exchange controls, though at times very troublesome, resulted in a steady increase of foreign reserves, in particular holdings of United States dollars

The old Bank of Abyssinia, much respected in pre-war days—when you never went to the counter to cash your cheque, but sat, having a chat with the manager in his sanctum, while a messenger brought your money, with a low bow—was put into liquidation by the Italians and never resuscitated. During the first days of the Emperor's return, Barclay's Bank stepped nobly into the breach and served all the needs of a community of diverse interests. Now we

The Royal car with mouted escort leaves the palace on 'flag day' and is held up by school girls selling flags

have the State Bank of Ethiopia—a very flourishing concern —about which the facts speak for themselves.

Since its foundation in August 1942 its assets have grown from Eth.$12,000,000 to Eth.$317,000,000 at the end of 1953. In 1953 its gross earnings amounted to Eth.$5,800,000, and at the end of that year its monetary reserves amounted to Eth.$181,800,000 and total deposits of Eth.$103,800,000. An indication of the growing prosperity of the people and of the interesting use of the bank as a medium of savings is the steady rise from year to year of the savings and time deposit accounts, which amounted to Eth.$8,200,000. As a further index to economic well-being it may be noted that Ethiopia has a favourable balance of trade. In 1953 the surplus reached a record of Eth.$44,100,000, of which 86 per cent was earned in gold or United States dollars.

Another step was to secure loans from external resources, and these have been accorded in generous measure. The Export and Import Bank of Washington supplied Eth.$6,805,602, of which a considerable amount has been repaid. The International Bank for Reconstruction and Development has given three loans aggregating Eth.$21,250,000, for highway construction and maintenance, financing the Development Bank of Ethiopia, and the development of telecommunication; of which Eth.$16,148,862 has been withdrawn and is still outstanding. There is also a United States Lend Lease (silver) loan of Eth.$9,629,375 still outstanding. Various other smaller loans have all been repaid in full.

Not only has help from abroad been in the form of loans. The World Health Organization and the Food and Agricultural Organization of the United Nations have provided technical staff and equipment which have been of considerable assistance; and a general Point Four Agreement, signed in 1951 with the Government of the U.S.A., has made possible the realization of plans for agricultural and educational development of the highest importance to this country. These plans include the establishment of an agricultural college and schools; the investigation of the water resources of the country; programmes of technical and scientific research and education; handicraft training; a public health project; the establishment of research stations; the initiation of agricultural extension work and assistance to the F.A.O. work already started, in vaccinating cattle.

Now to see what all these things have meant in strengthening the Government's power to realize its programme, let us compare their budgets at the beginning and end of the ten years under review. For the year ending September 1945 the estimated revenue was Eth.$38,072,000 and the estimated expenditure Eth.$37,942,000. For the year ending September 1954 (the latest for which figures are available) the estimated revenue was Eth.$121,340,000 and the estimated expenditure Eth.$121,295,606. You find, as you would expect, that the expansion in revenue of Eth.$83,000,000 is mainly due to the following: loans Eth.$13,250,000; increase in customs Eth.$40,250,000; and income tax Eth.$13,500,000.

When you come to expenditure you find that the expansion of Eth.$87,000,000 can be attributed to an increase of over Eth.$26,000,000 in expenditure upon the armed forces (including the Imperial Air Force); an increase of at least Eth.$9,000,000 on construction and maintenance of roads and bridges; an increase of Eth.$11,500,000 on education; of Eth.$3,000,000 on health services; of Eth.$6,500,000 for federal expenses in Eritrea; of over Eth.$1,000,000 in contributions to Point Four activities; and finally extraordinary expenditure amounting to Eth.$21,000,000, which included such items as subscriptions to the capital of the Imperial Communications Board and the Development Bank of Ethiopia, and expenditure on railways, ports and lights, and public buildings in Eritrea, and repayment of loans.

All this goes to show that there is money available for the realization of the Emperor's long-term programme of development, that the Government is meeting its obligations, and that there is growing prosperity amongst the people. As the State Bank's *Ethiopian Survey* of November 1954 says: 'Ethiopia's economy is extremely sound.'

14

The Next Ten Years

2. Communications

THAT the stability of the Government and the development of the resources of the country depend upon good communications needs no emphasis. The Emperor had already begun to tackle the problem before the Italian invasion, and since his return it has been in the forefront of his programme. Problem indeed it is, for the nature of the country, where the road may in a few miles climb the heights of the mountains and plunge again into the deep ravines—and this not once but many times in a day's journey—makes the solution difficult and costly. Add to this the climate, alternating between the torrential scouring rains of August and September and the wind-swept dryness of October that cracks and scars. The roads too are not for car and lorry alone, they are crossed and trampled by the many animals that graze alongside them or travel along them to market and fair.

The new factor that has enormously eased the situation has been the possibilities opened up by the introduction of air services—at a relatively low cost. It is amusing to watch the local services that ply between Addis Ababa and almost all the outlying provinces load and unload. Here is an old priest from Gondar come down to lay his case before the Abuna in Addis Ababa. With his bundle and his prayer stick he climbs out of the plane that has brought him in a few hours over mountain and valley, river and desert; a journey that twenty years ago would have taken him six weeks of wearisome walking with his mule or donkey to carry his luggage, and a boy to beat them along and enhance his prestige at the same time. The £10 he has paid for his trip would have been eaten up and more by the two travellers and their beast, even if time itself were of no value. Or here comes the Jimma plane and the merchant with his bags of coffee that would have needed a caravan for a fortnight to bring in the load over the steep Omo gorge and up through the long marshy plains where the Hawash spreads out in flood during the rainy season. Ethiopia is essentially air-minded. These services have been made possible by an agreement with Trans-World Air-lines whereby they furnish management and technical assistance, including air crews, for a period of seven years. Thus Ethiopia Air-lines Inc. was born and regular flights began in April 1946. The service has been a marked success. Fast Convair air-liners are used on the international routes between Addis Ababa, Nairobi, and several Middle East cities; and Douglas twin-engined planes cover a network of internal lines serving twenty-three towns within the Ethiopian Empire. There has been no fatality on the ninety million passenger miles flown to date. The fleet at present numbers twelve, and is to be added to shortly, as the planes are being increasingly used for freight, and the demands made on the services are more than can be met.

Ethiopian pilots and radio-operators are being trained in preparation for the time when American staff will be withdrawn. The initial financing of the Ethiopian Air-lines was assisted by a loan of Eth.$324,089 from Air Fleets Inc., which loan has been repaid in full.

The Franco-Ethiopian Railway has since the war greatly increased its rolling stock and general equipment, and made a thorough overhaul of its bridges and permanent way, which sustained considerable damage during the campaign. It can now carry a traffic of over half a million tons, three times more than its capacity before the war. Since federation considerable sums have been spent on the Eritrean railway connecting Asmara with the port at Massowah, on which port substantial improvements have been made. In the other direction the railway connects with services across the Sudan frontier to Kassala and Khartoum.

The great task of the maintenance, repair, and improvement of the empire's road system has by no means yet been accomplished, and many roads are still in a very poor state. But matters were speeded up in 1950 by a loan from the International Bank of U.S.$6,000,000; finally an Imperial Highway Authority was set up, financed in part by the World Bank, and in part by the Government, to assume control and responsibility for the work. The Authority 'has quite properly concentrated its attention on the main trunk roads, and in particular upon the road from Assab. This port is likely in the future to become the main outlet from the country.

The upkeep of the secondary roads so essential to the economic development of the country has so far baffled solution. The enormous Italian *trente-quatro* diesel lorries, which trundle with a sort of ponderous inevitableness to the innermost recesses of the country, collecting produce and distributing the counterpart of consumer goods, create havoc on these roads in wet weather. This makes it almost impossible for the Authority or the local government to keep pace with the maintenance that is necessary. It must be remembered that the Fascist Government spent £11,000 a mile on the construction of their road system. It is understood that the Government are contemplating an allocation of Eth.$5,000,000 a year for the upkeep of roads and bridges, but it is open to question whether this will suffice.

However, when all is said and done—and much is often

said by private owners of cars—the facts remain that the Government can now keep in touch with all parts of the empire by air; that in cases of emergency it can send the forces of law by wagon and lorry to reinforce at any point; that the produce of the country can be moved to the markets of the world by modern means of transport; that each week-end the town dwellers of Addis Ababa can drive their cars 50, 100, even 200 miles out to visit the most wonderful scenery. The barriers within and without are down. To those who can remember the six weeks' journey of forty years ago, before the capital could be reached from the outside world, or the eighteen days' journey of only twenty years ago; to those who saw the destruction of 1941, this is a miracle, the significance of which will be evident in relation to the future history of the country.

15

The Next Ten Years

3. *Security Forces*

E THIOPIA to-day is at peace. Public security reigns on the highways and byways of the empire. The Emperor has at his disposal a small but well-trained and adequately equipped army, and an efficient police force, capable of dealing with all foreseeable emergencies. Surely a cause for thankfulness in an uneasy world!

That this happy state of affairs would be achieved so comparatively quickly could certainly not have been taken for granted in early 1942, when the last of the British troops were withdrawn and Haile Selassie was left to face his responsibilities alone. The state of chaos within his country has already been described. It must be remembered too that the world was still at war—desperately at war—with the critical days after the fall of Singapore, and the struggle in the Western Desert, still to come. It was impossible to find equipment other than that available from the defeated enemy. Men's thoughts and energies were turned elsewhere in the common struggle for existence. Yet there were many problems for the Emperor to face in his own country and many question marks as to the future on his frontiers, all requiring—for the safety of his country and the peace of his own mind—that he should have the force at his back to ensure law and order at home and respect abroad.

It was under these circumstances, and with these limitations, that the Emperor set to work to plan the formation and organization of his security forces—the Regular Army, the Imperial Bodyguard (which has always been the prerogative of the King of Kings of Ethiopia), and the police.

The reorganization of the army was undertaken with the help —under the terms of the Agreement signed between Great Britain and Ethiopia in January 1942—of a British Military Mission composed of officers and non-commissioned officers. It was decided that at first the task should be dealt with by two separate administrations. The formation, training, and administration of the new Regular Army was to be the business of the British Military Mission and carried out under their control; and the maintenance and administration of the existing troops, so to speak the 'irregular' army composed largely of patriots and formations raised hastily during the recent campaign, was to be under the direct control of the Ministry of War. This 'irregular' army was partly trained, and was to be employed on the important and essential task of maintaining internal security whilst the Regular Army was being formed and trained. This practical arrangement worked very well until in August 1944 the 'irregular' was assimilated into the Regular Army, the whole becoming the Imperial Army under the Imperial Ethiopian Ministry of War. During the next two years trained Ethiopian officers took over all the posts of command and administration from the British officers, these latter continuing in the position of advisers and inspectors or instructors until the British Military Mission was withdrawn in 1951.

The Imperial Army is organized after the British model in three divisions with their peace-time headquarters at Addis Ababa, Harar, and Dessie; and there is the usual subdivision into brigades and battalions disposed about the country at suitable points. There is artillery, an Armoured Corps (recently equipped with more modern tanks), a Signal Corps, a Corps of Engineers, and an Army Service Corps; and the usual auxiliary services. A special feature of the Signal Corps is that it is mainly recruited from orphan boys and children of soldiers, who are given a good education and strict training and are mustered as signallers when they become of age.

The Haile Selassie I Military Training College at Gannet, twenty-five miles west of Addis Ababa, is a very important part of the army's organization. It was first opened in 1932 under Swedish instructors; and during the Italian invasion most of the young cadets were killed in the fighting. It was reopened in 1942 for cadets who had already begun courses of instruction in Khartoum. The college, until the British Military Mission was withdrawn, was under their control. Over 2,000 officers have graduated from the fourteen cadet courses which have been held. Instructional and adminis- trative courses are also held there for subaltern officers re- commended by their unit commanders, as also senior officers' courses and staff courses.

Recently the army has been receiving military equipment of all sorts from the United States; and in accordance with an agreement made between the United States and Ethiopia in October 1953 an American Military Assistance Advisory Group is now in the country for the purpose of training the Army in the use of these most up-to-date weapons.

The training of the Imperial Bodyguard, a *corps d'élite* of some 5,000 men, has been carried out by officers of the Swedish Army. The bearing of these men on parade—and of course they take part on many ceremonial occasions—is very fine indeed; and the efficiency of their training has been proved in war. For the Emperor, jumping at all oppor- tunities to give practical aid to the causes of the United Nations, has maintained at full strength for the past four years a battalion in Korea. The rank and file of this unit have been mostly furnished by the Imperial Bodyguard, but the officers have been drawn from the Imperial Army as well as from the Guard. These troops have done extremely well and have won golden opinions from the American commanders under whom they have served. It must have been with peculiar pride and pleasure that the Emperor read the following citations. The first is a Distinguished Unit Citation dated 12th December 1952:

The First Kagnew Battalion, Imperial Ethiopian Expeditionary Force to Korea, is cited for outstanding performance of duty and extraordinary heroism in action against the enemy in the vicinity of Sam-Hyon, Korea, during the period of 16th September to 22nd September 1951. Throughout the day and night of 16th September, the battalion, occupying defensive positions in close proximity to a large hostile force, dispatched a series of probing patrols in an effort to gather information as to the disposition of the enemy. Several contacts were made. . . . Finally an enemy force was observed preparing positions on the slope of a commanding terrain feature, and the battalion immediately sent two reinforced squads to assault the hill. Fighting with great determination, the friendly troops battled their way up the slope and drove the enemy from their positions with heavy casualties. With the objective secured, observers, utilizing their new vantage point, discovered feverish enemy activity on adjacent slopes and called for an air strike and artillery and mortar fire. After the initial bombardment, assaulting elements of the battalion hit the positions in a whirlwind attack, engaged the foe in hand-to-hand combat, and inflicted exceptionally heavy casualties upon the enemy. . . . The Kegnew Battalion . . . displayed such superlative effectiveness in accomplishing its mission as to set it apart and above other units participating in the action. The extraordinary heroism, determination of purpose, and magnificent fighting spirit of the members of this battalion reflect great credit on themselves and are in keeping with the most esteemed traditions of the military profession.

The second Distinguished Unit Citation is dated 26th June 1954:

The Third Kagnew Battalion, Ethiopian Expeditionary Forces to Korea, is cited for outstanding performance of duty and extraordinary heroism in action against the enemy in the vicinity of Tokan-Ni, Korea, on 20th May 1953. Following an intense mortar and artillery barrage which had sealed supply and reinforcement routes, the enemy launched a furious reinforced attack against two friendly outposts and the battalion's forward positions on the main line of resistance. The superior numbers of the attacking force would have impelled a lesser defender to withdraw to positions along a secondary line of defence; however, the battalion troops rallied with a magnificent surge of spirit and heroic determination to hold the assigned sector at any cost. The battalion called for the fire of their supporting artillery on the besieged first outpost and the men defending that position left their bunkers and moved through their own barrage to hurl the enemy from the outpost at bayonet point. This same procedure was followed by the second outpost and they too were successful in forcing the enemy to retreat. Meanwhile the hostile force hurled wave after wave against the main line of resistance in their attempt to overrun the battalion position but each time the defenders unhesitatingly raced from their positions to grapple with the enemy in hand-to-hand combat and, after exacting extremely heavy casualties, forced them to retreat. Due to the unwavering courage of the officers and men of the battalion every thrust of the enemy attack was repulsed and the entire invading force was decisively routed. . . . The superb *esprit de corps* and extraordinary heroism displayed by the members of this unit reflect great credit on themselves, their organization, and the Ethiopian Army.

No one can say that the new-model Ethiopian Army has not begun well.

The internal security of the country is primarily the responsibility of the Minister of the Interior, to whom in turn each Governor-General of a province is responsible for the maintenance of security in his own province. To enable them to carry out their responsibilities there is a centrally organized and administered State Police Force numbering some 24,000 officers and men, under the command of a Commissioner of Police. This large force has of course been gradually expanded from smaller beginnings; and has been trained and at first administered by experienced British police officers. The role of these British officers is now advisory only, and their numbers have been reduced. The range of effectiveness of the Imperial Police now reaches all but the remotest and most sparsely populated parts of the country and they are organized into 793 police stations covering 83 districts. The replacement of the old irregular police by their modern counterpart has led to prompter reporting of crime and to greater co-operation with the public in the maintenance of law and order. The healthy effect on security is already evident. That so large and efficient a force should have been brought into being in not much more than a dozen years is a remarkable achievement.

16

The Next Ten Years

4. Social Services

'EVERYONE who loves Ethiopia should concern himself with the founding of schools.'

'In order to strengthen this partnership in the League of Nations we must increase the number of our schools.'

'No one can doubt that the children of Ethiopia are lovers of learning and that their hands are open to receive education.'

'Knowledge is a treasure that must be grasped.'

I have chosen some sentences from speeches delivered by the Regent during the years 1925–30. They are indicative of his feelings at that time of the supreme necessity for the education of his people. They were spoken at school openings, or prize-givings, at which he was a regular visitor. There is no sphere of public activity in which his interest is more keenly shown, nor in which his personal influence is more deeply felt.

It was contact with Europe that first made Ras Makonnen insist on education for his son. It was perhaps a visit to Europe in 1924 that made that son resolve to bring education to his people. He had visited most of the western capitals, Rome, Paris, London, and Stockholm, and was determined to bring the fruits of western civilization to the knowledge of his own countrymen. With the entry also of Ethiopia into the League of Nations he was stimulated to still further efforts, to see that his country should not be judged lacking in the realm of knowledge and culture. It was after five years spent in exile, in England, that he returned the more determined still to open the path to higher education.

What then were the possibilities of education before the Regent took up the cudgels on its behalf? In the early part of the twentieth century these were threefold: Church, Mission, and State. The arrangement is chronological. During preceding centuries education, of a very primitive type and confined almost exclusively to the priestly caste, had been given by the churches. Outside each thatched church there would gather round the priest or scribe a sprinkling of the sons of the upper class and of the local clergy, to learn by rote the Psalms of David, in the ancient Ethiopic language (Geez). After the psalms would come the study of the gospels—but all in a language that the boys themselves did not understand and might never learn. Even the priests who read the service in Geez might only have a very slight idea of what they were reading.

The actual mechanics of reading and writing thus acquired in the church precincts, the clever boy would then make use of them to enable him to read and understand the more secular Amharic; but it is obvious that education of this kind is a very restricted affair and that it was only the boy of marked intelligence or perseverance who could translate his knowledge into everyday usefulness.

When, therefore, the missions started work in Ethiopia education was one of the first tasks to which they brought assistance. The schools started by the Swedish Mission in Harar and Addis Ababa have been the early training-ground of many of Ethiopia's best public men; and it was undoubtedly these and other mission schools that were the means of supplying the Emperor with some of the junior grades of that civil service which he so badly needed, and indeed still needs.

When, however, in 1908 Menelek opened the school which still bears his name, and this was enlarged and then in 1929 duplicated by the opening of the Tafari Makonnen School, there became available a steady stream of young Ethiopians who had received a good primary education and had also studied a foreign language—English, French, or Italian. Of these the most intelligent were then selected for further education abroad, and in 1935 some forty young men were actually undergoing training in various foreign countries and for many different vocations.

Sad to relate, it was many of these young men who lost their lives in the massacre that followed the attempt on Graziani's life in February 1937. It is the deliberate extermination of the young intelligentsia of that time that has caused the shortage of senior members of the civil service, who are badly needed.

All this expense of education abroad was, before the Italian aggression, provided for by the Regent from his private purse. There was plenty of good material ready to hand in this slowly awakening country, and the experience gained in those early years was of happy augury for the future. It was amplified and stimulated during the four years that the Emperor spent in exile. As I have said, he was far from idle in those years, gathering all the time knowledge of men and affairs. With his own family of sons and grandchildren in the very midst of their educational years, he must have visited many schools all over the country, and with his keenly critical mind selected and appraised systems and methods.

When the Emperor returned to his capital he was faced with two major problems in education. Except in a very few districts where the Italians had, of set policy, encouraged schools among the Moslem elements of the population, there was nothing. The Fascist policy had been to nullify what had been accomplished between 1925 and 1935 and to deny education to all but a minimum of Ethiopia's youth. There were no pupils in school, and worse still there were no teachers.

Within a year the Emperor had reopened the Tafari Makonnen School with an American missionary, his wife, and fifteen-year-old daughter as foreign staff, and a group of Ethiopians—priests, deacons, and older men who could start off with the rudiments of reading, writing, and arithmetic. A Greek trader taught geography—within a month 1,000 pupils had enrolled themselves.

The other problem was how to help those boys and girls who had escaped the Fascist oppression and either in Palestine, Egypt, or Kenya had, during the years of exile, found the opportunity of elementary education and had now come back to their own country and found nothing to meet their more advanced needs. These boys and girls were keenly desirous to continue where they had left off; and though the British Council, which had established a centre in Addis Ababa in 1942, and others, were able to offer temporary help, it was clear that there was enough material available to make the beginnings of a secondary school. An old agricultural college, built by the Italians about five miles outside Addis Ababa, was secured and put in some sort of order. In little more than two years after the Emperor's return the British Council had produced a headmaster from the staff of its institute, text-books for the teachers had been contributed, forms, desks, chairs had been hastily constructed, and in 1945 His Majesty cut the ribbon across the door and led us around the new Haile Selassie I Secondary School. Three of its first pupils have now taken their honours degree at Oxford.

From these simple, yet far from easily achieved beginnings, education has spread with almost incredible rapidity. Advice has been sought from many sources, teachers have been imported from many countries. The criticism might be levelled that there is lack of continuity in the policy adopted for the schools; that a system cannot be consistent which has Americans, Canadians, British, Indians, all with their own very varied ideas on just as varied educational ideals. The curriculum in the hands of this international group has as its academic bourne the General Certificate of Education of the University of London, though there are many offshoots into technical and commercial branches leading to internal diplomas. Yet there is much to be said for the point of view that the Ethiopian is seeking to establish his own system, and that only by experimenting with many will he find the one most suited to his own needs. So may the present kaleidoscope settle down to the pattern that is their final choice.

Another secondary school bearing the name of General Orde Wingate was established some two years later on the other side of the town. This has a British staff and headmaster and, like the Haile Selassie Secondary School, gives all its instruction in English, though there are of course Ethiopian teachers for Amharic subjects. This school has received considerable assistance in staffing from the British Council but is gradually coming under the full control of the Government. Secondary sections have also been formed in some of the larger elementary schools.

In this way, and as quickly as he may, the Emperor is slowly building up the ranks of the civil service and ministries as well as those of the banks and commercial concerns. Ethiopian youth learns its trade quickly, even if for the moment and perforce somewhat superficially, and wherever you may go you can see them in bank and office, in the shops and on the lorries. All are keen and deadly serious but, as is natural, with no conception of scholarship or craftsmanship. These are later developments that can only come as the background of their lives expands, and open competition in a wider market, both academic and manual, becomes available to them.

Activities in the educational sphere have thus been developed and are developing at the moment along many lines. To quote from the handbook to Ethiopia:

> The normal 8-grade Primary Course, and there are some 70,000 children now enrolled in schools all over the country, culminates in the National General Certificate examination, on the basis of which students are selected for different types of secondary schooling; these are five in number—Academic, Commercial, Technical, Agricultural, and Teaching Training. In such cases the education is free of cost to the student and is arranged to cover four years. Free boarding accommodation is provided for students from distant homes.

The foundation of the University College of Addis Ababa in 1950 'came as a further logical step in the expansion of Ethiopia's educational system.' This college, which accepts students who have completed their school certificate in four subjects, provides opportunities for advanced studies which have been formerly only possible overseas. The aim of the college is to prepare students 'to continue professional studies abroad, or later at the Haile Selassie I University now in the course of construction.' After a four years' course is completed the college awards Bachelor of Arts and Bachelor of Science degrees.

An engineering college, developing from the technical school of earlier days, which now functions as a secondary school, and destined to be an integral part of the University, was opened in September 1952 under the name of the College of Technology—and again the General School Certificate was recommended as the condition of entry. Up to date it is not possible to secure enough candidates with this qualification, and other preparatory courses have been arranged to bridge the gap in numbers, until sufficient candidates can present themselves; at present it is arranged that after two years of instruction qualified students shall proceed to the U.S.A. to complete their education.

The Commercial School, which has been in existence for some years, trains boys and girls in secretarial and commercial subjects. Students are accepted from the upper grades of the primary, and from any grade in the secondary schools, and may work either for the special certificate awarded by the Ministry of Education or for the examination of the Royal Society of Arts, London. About 150 students attend this school, and many of those who have passed through it are already in good positions in the State Bank, the ministries, and many business institutions. There have been one or two attempts to start an agricultural eollege that shall give a training suitable for those who wish to promote what is surely at present the most important branch, potentially, of the country's resources. Now there has been established at Jimma, to the south-west of Addis Ababa, an Agricultural Technical School, under the auspices of the Ministry of Education and the Point Four (T.C.A.) Basic Agreement for a Co-operative Agricultural Educational Programme. This was opened for the admission of 70 students in October 1952, and has proved a great success, both practically and in securing the interest of other intending students, over 700 of whom have now applied for admission. So far the school is of secondary school level, and is planned to cover four years' instruction both theoretical and practical. There is a small agricultural college now restarted at Ambo in the province of Shoa.

Lastly, but surely to serve the most important and pressing of all the country's needs, comes the Teachers' Training College, first opened with assistance from the British Council in securing staff, in 1944 at Addis Ababa It has now been

Tony Boyadjian

The Emperor visits a girls' school ; the arithmetic lesson

Tony Boyadjian

The Emperor sets in motion an electric drill at the Sinclair Petroleum
Company's exploratory survey station in Somaliland

moved to Harar, where more accommodation is available, and with a view to expansion. But there is difficulty in finding enough would-be teachers to fill the ever growing need, and there is always a dangerous yearly loss of teachers to other professions. These are urgent problems which have to be faced if education is to go on expanding as it should.

Here then are the different types of secondary and advanced education already in being—some are still very young, and it is the students of the present day who will make the traditions and the character of these various schools. But the initiative, the guiding hand, the inspiration have come from the Emperor. Education is the interest nearest to the Emperor's heart, as all who work with him know. He has been well served. Teachers and administrators—they are gathered from among seventeen nations this year—are fully aware of his intense personal interest in every school, in every college; and not only in education as a policy, but in the welfare of the individual children, boys and girls, who are in the schools. He comes to see them, often at their sports or their performances—but often also without fore-warning, and unostentatiously; he goes into their class-rooms, to their dining-room; he asks questions about their food and their comfort; he listens to their complaints; he brings them fruit during the fast from his own orchards. At the annual prize-giving he gives them their awards with his own hands; they come to greet him at his palace—all of them—on his birthday. He invites them at Christmas to receive their annual gift jersey. He talks to them, he thinks and plans for them. He personally selects many of those who go abroad to complete their education.

He is broad-minded enough to know that girls should have an equal chance with boys. The Itege (Empress) Menan School for girls is almost as old as the Tafari Makonnen School for boys—and the opportunities offered to girls are, on paper, exactly similar to those for boys, though in practice this does not bear the fruit that it might. The Christian influence is never more clearly shown than in the equality of opportunity for boys and girls, men and women, and the following excerpts from various statements made by the Emperor on education may serve to show the viewpoint from which he looks into the future.

Education of the youth is the surest guarantee of a better life. Therefore among the many projects undertaken for the welfare and prosperity of Ethiopia we have planned that education be the principal. . . .

Agricultural and industrial pursuits are the main avenue to the development of our country. It is not possible to follow these pursuits only by mere desire to do so; for desire alone cannot bring achievement; to bring this desire to fruition education is necessary. Education is therefore the great need of our country. No real progress could be made without it—without it the national wealth cannot increase—without it our work cannot advance. It is therefore really necessary to strive for education and for the success which it ensures. . . .

Loyalty inspires understanding, and understanding co-opera-tion; these are the clearest evidences of strength. But the solid basis for all lies in education. It is education which allows people to live together, makes them avoid the pitfalls of immor-ality, and induces respect for the law. Truly the attainment of these high aims is based on education, the helping of people to live together, avoid indulgence, immorality, and lawlessness. . . .

To command and be commanded is the fruit of education: unity and confidence is the result. Moreover, you will have to cultivate your minds: you can then defend yourselves by this armour of education, and be able to make your own decisions without being misled by contrary opinions which might lead you to error. . . .

In addition to the founding of these many schools and colleges a most important adjunct to education was the opening in 1944 of the National Library. This not only contains a general library which, from its original collection of mainly Italian books, has through gifts, and as funds and circumstances have permitted, come to possess a very cosmopolitan collection of books; but is also the museum in which old manuscripts, historical treasures, and a collection of books about Ethiopia are kept.

For the few occasional readers who used it at the beginning it has grown to attract numbers of readers daily. There is a large reading-room as well as a magazine-room; lectures are held at regular intervals. It was on the opening of this that the Emperor spoke words which are clear evidence of his own attitude towards education in its broader aspect:

We must remember that the full measure of a library is not to be calculated simply by the numbers of those who use it. A good and honest mind assimilating knowledge and gaining inspiration from study may be of the greatest service to the future generations who come into this building to gain more knowledge or a wider inspiration. As the Apostle Paul has pointed out to us, it is not enough simply to read and to mark. The criterion of honest learning is the inward digestion of what has been studied.

Opinions which spring from superficial reading—the glib use of a glib word culled from desultory turning of pages in a book— may be a great danger to right progress. Let us earnestly recommend to those who will come to use this library that they avoid this superficial knowledge. . . . In the present terrible situation in the world to-day it is perhaps with special pleasure and hope that we open this library. It is of some inspiration for the future and for our hopes in peace to recall that what is highest in human achievement has got its interest beyond mere geographical boundaries. The world of a library is the world of knowledge. The world of knowledge of the search after truth. It is a world which is truly international.

Finally, as he unveiled the statue commemorating the murder of one of the bishops, Abuna Petros, who died rather than betray his country:

As you all know, before Ethiopia was invaded by the enemy we had done all that could be done to advance education in spite of all the difficulties that had to be encountered.

Humanity by nature is gifted to think freely, but in order that this free thought should lead him to the goal of liberty and independence, his way of thinking must be shaped by process of education. It is understood that the independence of mind created by education individually will have as a result the creation of independently minded nations.

When we compare the numbers of schools functioning in Ethiopia to-day, we can view with keen satisfaction the advance achieved within the past five years. . . .

Education, work, diligence are the main foundations of our national existence. We call upon all Ethiopians to send their children to the nearest school, for it is suicide, and a crime against responsibility which God places in all parents, not to educate one's own children.

The catastrophe which was brought about by human hand during the past years can be avoided in the future by religion and hope in God which should be in the heart of the people. All this can be achieved by education which if not borne by the youth, the effort which is made for peace will be in vain.

Next to education—the well-being of the mind—comes the Emperor's care for health and welfare. In the light of progress and achievement it is interesting to note the changes that have taken place in the capital and in the country, and to compare the situation in 1920 with that in 1955.

When he became Regent in 1916 there was little to show of medical, health, or welfare services throughout the country. In Addis Ababa there was one hospital, which had originally been equipped and staffed by a special Russian

Mission at the time of the battle of Adowa. Then the Government engaged French doctors and others, who were assisted by nuns from the Catholic Mission. It served perhaps one in a thousand of the town's population. There was hardly a trained nurse in the whole of Ethiopia and no facilities for Europeans except the services of private doctors. There was nothing to be done in those days but to rally the community (there were just thirteen British Europeans) and to take turns whether trained or not to nurse the sick. I well remember during my first few months in Addis Ababa assisting the English doctor at a confinement, doing night duty on a case of puerperal insanity, and sitting one whole afternoon with a patient suffering from D.T.

It was obvious with the growing Ethiopian population as well as the advent of Europeans, whose numbers were rapidly increasing, that facilities must be increased and improved. The arrival of American Presbyterian missionaries from the west, where they had started some medical work, instigated the Emperor to issue an invitation to them to build and staff a hospital in Addis Ababa. The result was the George Memorial Hospital, built on a site provided by the Emperor, but financed, equipped, and staffed by the Women's Board of the Presbyterian Mission. This was followed by a second hospital set up by the Seventh Day Adventist Mission, which later became a memorial to the Empress Zauditu and dealt mainly with maternity cases. Both these hospitals were first-class, and Europeans as well as Ethiopians found them kind, competent, and helpful.

The Emperor took a keen interest in the building of these hospitals, going down often to inspect, staying to watch operations in the theatre, paying visits to the patients in the wards. It was an interest which he passed on to his younger daughter Princess Tsahai, who later, when in exile in England, trained at Guy's Hospital and assisted at the Great

Ormond Street Hospital for Children. It was a cruel stroke of fortune not only for her sorrowing parents but also for her country when she died. It was not only her qualifications but the activity and vigour of her personality that had been so valuable to her country.

Since the war an ante-natal clinic has been set up in her memory by her own countrywomen, and a fine hospital, largely built with the moneys of the English people who had known, heard of her, and respected her.

A leprosarium—the work of the Sudan Interior Mission— was opened in 1934 with a Canadian doctor and staff of twelve nurses. Eighty inmates were admitted and others treated at the clinic attached to it.

All these were in the main the work of missionary societies who saw and met the crying need for help. But as proof, if necessary, of his own realization of the need for further medical assistance to his people, the Regent opened in 1926 the Bethsaida Hospital, which was founded and maintained by his private purse. Though its buildings and equipment were on a small scale, fine work was done by the Swedish doctor in charge of it, with his two Swedish sisters. One of the great services they rendered was the training of Ethiopian women as competent and intelligent nurses.

Meanwhile, clinics were started, first by the municipality and police, a Pasteur institute was founded and maintained, and the Italians built a hospital which they handed to the Emperor, 'as a token of friendship,' in 1934. Everything had his ready support and approval. Now, twenty years later, we can look on that picture and on this.

The Menelek Hospital has been almost entirely rebuilt; the Bethsaida with its two small blocks, capable of holding 30 beds, has been transformed into the Haile Selassie I Hospital of 160 beds, with an international staff. The hospital given by the Italians has been named the Ras Desta after the Princess Tenagne Worq's husband whom they killed. The Russian Government have equipped and staffed the Dejach Balcha. The Princess Tsahai hospital stands as a fitting memorial to the young princess. Staffed mainly by British doctors, matron, and sisters it has within the last few years trained its first group of Ethiopian women nurses.

In the poor market district of the town stands the St Paul Hospital under a Yugoslav director and staff, and here treatment is free. The hospital is maintained from the Emperor's privy purse as his personal charity.

There are in addition many clinics, notably that in Addis Ababa for women and children outside the Tekla Haimanot Church in the busy market area. Directed by an indefatigable woman doctor it deals with an average of 300 cases daily. This is only one of 150 scattered up and down the country and staffed in many cases by Ethiopian dressers who have received an elementary training in Addis Ababa.

In the same way provincial hospitals have been established in most of the larger towns; the total number functioning in Ethiopia is forty-six, and the number of patients treated in both hospitals and clinics during the year 1952–3 was well over half a million.

The leprosarium opened in 1934 with its eighty inmates has grown to house 1,300, who are being treated through the large supply of silfatron received from the World Health Organization, who sent out a specialist to survey the situation. Meanwhile four other centres for the treatment of the disease have been established in outlying parts of the empire.

Enough has been said to show that the provision for the treatment of the sick has during the Emperor's lifetime increased and improved beyond all possible expectation.

But apart from actual treatment much has been done to

combat disease. The 'Institut Pasteur d'Ethiopia' has extended its services to cover the production of vaccines against smallpox, typhus, rabies, and cholera. An entomologist attached to the institute has made mosquito investigations, and anti-malarial campaigns have been set in motion; a centre has been established for venereal disease treatment; in co-operation with W.H.O. and with support from the United Nations International Children's Emergency Fund a widespread B.C.G. vaccination campaign is being carried on to combat tuberculosis. Special anti-epidemic teams are ready for service as need arises in any district.

The training of nurses continues at four hospitals and some of these trainees have already received their diplomas and licenses as fully trained nurses. A few have been sent abroad for further education and some five of these have now returned to take positions in the various hospitals.

Finally there has been established at Gondar a Medical College and a Public Health Training Centre under the joint auspices of the Ministry of Public Health, the United States Operations Mission (Point Four), the W.H.O., and the U.N.I.C.E.F. Here Public Health Officers are to be trained whose duties will be a combination of doctor, sanitary inspector, and health educator.

To all these activities is lent the personal interest of the Emperor. You may meet him any afternoon driving through the town, only the flag flying on his car to warn you who is passing; and you know he has been to see something— school, hospital, clinic, new construction of building or road—to see with a practised eye whether it is progressing, to encourage, to reprimand, to exhort, to hasten. A visit is no idle survey; no organized reception with bouquets and speeches and whitewash—those are reserved for a special occasion. But there may be only half an hour's warning and then His Majesty is there, walking into every

Tony Boyadjian

The Empress visits the kindergarten of the school that she founded in 1927

room, talking to the individual child, sympathizing, observing, commenting, suggesting.   All is his own personal concern, with the result that he is not the remote autocrat, king within the four walls of his palace, but the true father of the people, his eye to see their needs, his ear to listen for their requests, his mind to plan, his purse to pay.

17

The Church

NO account of the Emperor would be complete without reference to the Church of which he is 'the unchallenged head,' that Church which has been referred to as the 'governing element' in Ethiopian society.

Christianity arrived in the country during the fourth century, when Frumentius hastened to Alexandria with news of his conversion of the King, and the care of his sons. From that moment the fortunes of King and State have been inextricably bound together, and at times the divinity of the royal state has been most prominently stressed.

Not much is known of the very early history of the Church, but it had a chequered career, and its influence was on the wane when in the thirteenth century, and largely owing to the zealous efforts of the Abuna Tekla Haimanot, who founded the monastery at Debra Libanos, some eighty miles north of the present capital, there was a revival of faith. A revision of the Bible was made; and the liturgy and church services took the form that they have to-day. Subjected to the fierce influence of the Portuguese Catholics the Church lost prestige, and needed a revival. This took place in the fifteenth century, when most of the hymns, anthems, and antiphons now in use in the services were composed and set down. There followed in the sixteenth century the invasion of the country by Ahmed Gran, when Christianity in the south, and even in parts of Shoa, was almost wiped out. For three centuries thereafter there was stagnation; and for the mass of the people religion tended to become a matter of outward form and superstition. The very fact that the leading ecclesiastic was always a foreigner, consecrated bishop by a foreigner in a far distant country, a priest who knew nothing of the life and customs of his flock, in a diocese far too large to be manageable, did not improve matters.

There were, of course, always the enlightened few, chiefly among the aristocracy who had been taught Geez—the early language of Church and State—who had studied their Bibles, and to whom religion was more than a formal habit. Such men deplored the state into which the Church had fallen, and among this number was the Emperor Menelek. During his reign an effort was made to stir the dull ashes of religion into a glowing force again. Foreign missions were encouraged to restart work in the country in the hope that their influence might lead to improvement. The text of the Bible became available in Amharic, through the agency of the British and Foreign Bible Society, who had published a translation as long ago as 1840.

Ras Tafari Makonnen as Regent had continued this policy of encouragement to missionary bodies and made good use of their medical and educational work, regarding this no doubt as a good method of spreading general education and reform. But his real concern was in the improvement of the Ethiopian Church, and he went much deeper into this task. He believes that it is essential that Ethiopia should stand before the whole world as clearly and unequivocally a Christian state under a Christian ruler. He believes that to make this a reality Church and State must be more closely bound together, as in the old days. He is convinced that unless the Church is re-vitalized and re-enlightened to the point when it will command the respect and allegiance of the modern intelligent young men, there will be a tendency for Church and State to fall apart. He regards himself—as indeed he is—as the head of Church and State. It is therefore his responsibility to ensure that progress inside the Church should keep pace with progress in the State.

In his approach to this problem—delicate because the Church is strongly entrenched in its own conservatism and in the superstitious awe which it commands from the people—the Emperor has shown great wisdom. He has relied on personal example and gentle persuasion rather than on measures for forcing the pace which might lead to a derogatory attitude towards the Church. An example will illustrate his method. The traditional ceremonies connected with death and the commemoration of the departed were a considerable burden on the poorer members of society. 'Those who have money,' says Walker,

will hold a commemoration on the third, seventh, twelfth, fortieth, and eightieth day, and after six months and one year and seven years. . . . On the third day there is the taskar of the 'salist' when even if one is poor, he must bring three baskets of bread, six pots of beer, and six dishes of sauce for the priests, and a load of wood for the kindling of the fire. Also there will be money for the Absolution—two or seven dollars and a few raisins, and two or three tapers. Therefore if a man has not the dollars he must perforce call a surety and borrow them. Nor is bread alone fitting for a commemoration and a poor man must provide at least one pot of beer for the poor, one for the head of the Church, one for the chamberlain, and three pots for the priests; so also six dishes of sauce whether of meat or of vegetables, with a hundred pieces of bread. Else he may not make a commemoration.[1]

The excerpt will show what a heavy charge this was to the poor man; yet respect for the dead, and superstitious awe of the Church and the monks, and considerations of prestige compelled observance. The only people to gain by all this were the priests.

[1] Walker: *The Abyssinian at Home.*

When Ras Tafari's second daughter died in 1932 he issued a short statement. In it he declared his view that the traditional forty days' mourning was unreasonably and unnecessarily long, and was a cause of hardship and unwarrantable expense to the poor. He therefore was ordering a period of three days' mourning only for his own daughter and he hoped that the Church authorities would succeed in bringing in this innovation. This made a great impression and met with general acceptance.

He has worked steadily all his life to bring the Scriptures and the Church services to the knowledge of the people. He took the first steps toward this as soon as he became Regent. An edition of the Gospels with an Amharic commentary on the ancient Geez was published; the liturgy with an Amharic translation in parallel columns was brought out; and the same was done for the baptism service. A translation of the Gospels and Acts was made by the late Belatingeta Herowi with the Regent's active encouragement; and in 1936 an Amharic translation of the whole Bible was completed. He let it be known that he thought it would be a good thing if an Amharic text of the Bible was kept in every church throughout the land. This was not an order, but, put that way, the thing was done. The head priest of our own parish church came to us and said that as Ras Tafari had recommended them to get an Amharic Bible, would we please get them one, and a suitable box to keep it in!

Since the return of the Emperor in 1941 the use of Amharic in the churches has been greatly extended. The example was set in the Church of the Saviour of the World just outside the gates of the Emperor's palace, and also at the Church of the Trinity, which was built by the Emperor and is the mausoleum of the Imperial family. Here most of the religious services of special importance are held, and are conducted with great dignity and impressiveness. Amharic is mostly used. Special trouble has been taken, due to the Emperor's insistence, to raise the standard of preaching; on occasions, sermons are broadcast by the Addis Ababa wireless station.

A theological college was founded by the Emperor in the year 1944 for the training of priests. During the last three years there has been a growing demand for the emancipation of the Ethiopian Church from the control of the Egyptian Coptic Church and from its Patriarch at Alexandria. The Emperor has steadily pressed this claim to freedom.

When Abuna Mattheos died in 1926, an Egyptian, Abuna Cyril, was appointed Archbishop as usual, but as the result of representations by Ras Tafari, four Ethiopian monks were consecrated bishops by the Patriarch in Alexandria. A little later, while on a visit to Addis Ababa, the Patriarch consecrated a fifth. This was a great step forward.

The Italians during their occupation of the country were desirous of destroying all other foreign influence and wished to break this connection with Egypt. Abuna Querillos refused to co-operate with this policy, and left the country. They then made the old Abuna Abraha their instrument, and declared the independence of the Ethiopian Church in December 1937. The Abuna was declared the Metropolitan. The Patriarch's retort to this was to put the Church in Ethiopia under a ban of excommunication.

When the Emperor returned in 1941, he reopened negotiations with the Patriarch. Querillos returned to Ethiopia in June 1942 with a delegation from the Coptic Church, and the Patriarch lifted the ban of excommunication. The Patriarch Johannis died shortly after, and was succeeded by Macanis, who in June 1944 sent another delegation to Ethiopia, which took back a document setting forth the Ethiopian demands, of which the most important was that an Ethiopian should be chosen as Archbishop, to be consecrated

A religious ceremony outside the church at Axum

Priests, deacons, and acolytes accompany the 'ark' as it is carried out of church

by the Patriarch; that an Ethiopian synod should choose bishops and suffragans to be appointed by the Archbishop. These two demands were turned down flatly, but negotiations continued, and gradually the Coptic Church conceded the Ethiopian demands.

By the middle of 1948 it had been agreed that the Patriarch should consecrate five more Ethiopian bishops; that on the death of Querillos an Ethiopian should go to Cairo to be consecrated Archbishop by the Patriarch; and that thereafter this Archbishop should have authority to consecrate Ethiopian bishops, on the sole condition of informing the Patriarch beforehand of what he intended to do.

In October 1950 Abuna Querillos died, and the way was opened for the consecration of an Ethiopian Archbishop—and the choice fell, as was expected, on the Itchegi, who had already been consecrated bishop by the Patriarch under the name of Aba Basileos.

Throughout these negotiations the Emperor acted with his usual patience and perseverance, restraining his own people when they wished to break off negotiations and gain their ends without the consent of the Egyptians. He returned constantly to the charge as opportunity occurred. Looking back on it all, one sees that he recognized that under all the circumstances the Egyptians were playing a losing game; that, as before, time was on his side, and that if the Ethiopians bided their time they would gain their ends by consent, without a rupture in the continuity of the life of the Church. The link with Egypt will be maintained through the succession of the Archbishop.

A long patience, a far-seeing accommodation to passing circumstances, a resolute determination to make the most of every opportunity, this is the strength of the Head of State and Church in Ethiopia.

18

Eritrea

IT is not within the scope of this book to disentangle the chequered history of Eritrea. It is sufficient to say that from antiquity it was bound up with that of Ethiopia and belonged to the old kingdom of Axum. In the sixteenth century, however, the Turks took possession of Massowah, the outlet on the Red Sea; and in the latter half of the nineteenth century, when Turkish influence in that area waned, the Italians occupied that port in February 1885, having already bought the port of Assab, farther south, from an Italian commercial company who had purchased it as a trading station in 1869.

Eritrea is on the whole an unproductive country, for erosion has devastated the hillsides and the only really productive agriculture is in the deep and narrow valleys. It is divided amongst four main groups of peoples speaking different languages—the Christian agriculturists of the plateau, the Arab-Beja Mohammedans, nomads of the northern hills and western plains, the negroid communities of the south-west, and the Arab-Afar Mohammedan nomads of the south-east. Bound in the old days with Tigre and on the main trade routes to the Red Sea ports it had a natural economic stability, but isolated from these its position became wholly uneconomic.

The occupation of Massowah and the subsequent penetration inland by the Italians led naturally to wars with the Ethiopians, of which the most notable incident, after the Treaty of Ucciali, already mentioned, was the defeat of the Italians at the battle of Adowa. When the situation

stabilized after this battle, the frontiers of the Italian colony,
which in 1890 had been named Eritrea by the Italians, became
by mutual agreement those which still pertained at the outbreak of war in 1936. The name is derived from the Greek
name for the Red Sea mentioned in an early first-century
manuscript called *The Periplus of the Erythraean Sea*.

This arbitrary delimitation of the frontiers contained of
course the seeds of future war. The colony with its
frontiers established in 1896 contained a large slice of the
Ethiopian province of Tigre, which fact made irredentism on
the part of the Ethiopians inevitable. On the other hand the
Italians were faced with the unpleasant fact that Eritrea could
not be otherwise than a financial and economic burden to
them unless its boundaries were pushed out southwards to
include at least the rest of the province of Tigre; moreover
they nourished a burning desire to avenge the disaster of
Adowa.

After the conclusion of the war in 1941, when the Italians
had been expelled from both Ethiopia and Eritrea, decisions
as to the future of the Italian colonies in Africa had to await
the signature of a Peace Treaty with Italy. Meanwhile a
British caretaker administration of Eritrea was installed.
There is little doubt that if this delay could have been dis-
pensed with and a decision had been taken at once to hand
the whole territory over to Ethiopia this would have met with
general acceptance.

The Peace Treaty was eventually signed in Paris on 15th
September 1947. Under its terms Italy abandoned all right
and title to her former African colonies; and it was stipulated
that their final disposal should be determined jointly by the
Governments of the United Kingdom, the U.S.A., the
Soviet Union, and France, with the proviso that

if with respect to any of these territories the Four Powers are not
agreed upon their disposal within one year from the coming into

force of the Treaty of Peace with Italy, the matter shall be referred to the General Assembly of the United Nations for a
recommendation, and the Four Powers agree to accept the
recommendation and to give effect to it.

A fact-finding delegation, known as the Four Power Commission of Investigation, was dispatched to Eritrea by the
four powers concerned, but in the end they failed to agree
on a solution, and on 15th September 1948 they referred the
matter to the General Assembly for a recommendation as
provided.

On 21st November 1949 the General Assembly appointed
a United Nations Commission for Eritrea with instructions
to study the problem of Eritrea and to submit by 15th June
1950 proposals for its solution. The Commission visited
the territory, made exhaustive inquiries on the spot, con-
sulted all the Governments interested, and made its report
to the Assembly on 8th June 1950. The Commission was
composed of representatives of Burma, Norway, the Union
of South Africa, Guatemala, and Pakistan; the first three of
these agreed upon one set of conclusions; the other two
submitted differing ones.

Finally, six months later—to be precise on 2nd December
1950—after protracted discussions and lobbying, the General
Assembly of the United Nations adopted a resolution providing for the federation of Eritrea and Ethiopia under the
sovereignty of the Ethiopian Crown. It laid down that local
powers in the field of domestic affairs would be vested in the
Eritrean State; that jurisdiction over defence, foreign affairs,
currency and finance, foreign and interstate commerce, and
external and interstate communications, including ports,
were to be reserved to the Federal Government. A single
nationality was to prevail throughout the federation; and the
enjoyment of human rights and fundamental liberties was to
be safeguarded in respect of all residents. The portion of

the resolution laying down the foregoing provisions was to constitute the Federal Act. A later paragraph further provided that a constitution for Eritrea was to be drafted by a Commissioner appointed by the United Nations and submitted to a representative assembly of Eritreans chosen by the people. Finally the resolution determined that the Federal Act and the Constitution of Eritrea should enter into effect following ratification of the Federal Act by the Emperor of Ethiopia, and following approval by the Commissioner, adoption by the Eritrean Assembly and ratification by the Emperor of Ethiopia of the Eritrean Constitution.

All this came about. In his palace at Addis Ababa the Emperor Haile Selassie formally ratified the Federal Act on 11th September 1952. At sunset on 15th September the British flag was lowered in Asmara and the Ethiopian flag raised before an enormous crowd, and the federation came into being.

This baldly is the story, culled from official reports, of how the federation of Eritrea with Ethiopia came about. It was the fruit of five years of patient negotiation carried out on the whole in an atmosphere of restraint and calm.

From the beginning there were two solutions in the field—unification of Eritrea with Ethiopia or the complete independence of Eritrea. Later partition was proposed, but this suggestion found no favour with either Moslem or Christian. Really there was never any doubt that the solution would be unification—any other view was the result of either political bias or muddled thinking. That, at least, was the conviction of the Emperor and his friends. As usual he was prepared to bide his time, and his chief concern was that the solution should be one sponsored and approved by the United Nations. He and his Government would prefer complete unification, but if federation was the solution that would secure the blessing of the United Nations it should be accepted without reservation. He showed his confidence in the outcome by keeping himself in the background throughout the long negotiations, and leaving it to his Vice-Minister of Foreign Affairs, Ato Aklilu Habta Wald, to do all the talking and to press steadily the Ethiopian point of view.

There is no doubt that the successful result of the negotiations and the return of Eritrea to the motherland has enormously increased the Emperor's prestige amongst his own people. They regard it as the crowning achievement of a long life of endeavour in the service of his people.

In Eritrea the feeling at first was one of relief that a decision had been reached and general determination to make the new system work; and of expectancy, to see what the future would bring—they had not long to wait. On 4th October the Emperor Haile Selassie I crossed the River Mareb, the boundary between Ethiopia and Eritrea, and began a four weeks' tour in Eritrea. Significantly, on his way he stopped to visit the ancient city of Axum and Adowa.

At the river had assembled the leaders of the Eritrean people to greet Their Imperial Majesties. In reply to the speeches of welcome the Emperor said: 'By crossing the Mareb river we are doing away with the barrier which has for so long separated brother peoples,' and he went on to remind his listeners that in July 1940 when he came out from England to lead his people in the liberation of the country he had declared:

Whether on this side or on the other side of the Mareb join in the struggle by the side of your Ethiopian brothers to throw off the yoke of foreign domination! Your destiny is bound up with that of the rest of Ethiopia in the strictest sense of the word. I have come to restore the independence of my country, including Eritrea . . . whose people will henceforth dwell under the Ethiopian flag.

The seventy-mile drive from the frontier to the capital Asmara was, along its length, a heart-warming revelation of the welcome the people of Eritrea were prepared to give him—it was a triumph for his own personality as well as a sign that the solution of their problems had been accepted. On arrival at Asmara, Haile Selassie, before entering the palace, addressed the enormous crowd collected there to give him welcome. In a speech—which of set purpose was long and detailed because he felt that it was right that they should hear it from the Emperor's own mouth—he gave a sketch of Eritrean history from the earliest times; he set out fully the efforts he had himself made to secure unity; he pointed out that, even during the Italian occupation of Eritrea, Eritreans in large numbers had entered the service of the Ethiopian Government; that now barriers would be down and Ethiopian resources would be at the service of Eritrea; and, finally, he appealed to all Christians and Mohammedans, Eritreans, Ethiopians, and foreigners to sink their differences and unite in making the new order work for the welfare and prosperity of all.

In the succeeding days the Emperor visited every part of the country, including the port of Massowah and even the islands off the coast, moving freely among the people without obvious escort. A special pilgrimage was made by him to the cemetery at Keren where are buried the allied soldiers who lost their lives in the famous battle of 1941. In a most moving tribute he said: 'The soil on which we are now treading is soil sacred to the memory of thousands of families throughout the world whose beloved sons here fell in the cause of justice and freedom.' He went on to give a detailed description of the battle and mentioned by name the commanders and units who took part, and to comment on the many parts of the world from which help came; and he ended: 'We invoke the blessing of Almighty God on the heroes, named and nameless, of the battlefield of Keren, and now lay to their eternal memory our wreaths on these hallowed graves. This place we shall always respect, and devote our personal interest towards it.'

Wherever the Emperor went—and he went everywhere—he mingled freely with Christian, Mohammedan, Eritrean, and foreigner and stressed the need for unity and service, and there is no doubt his words created a great impression. The outstanding result of the visit was the growth of a feeling amongst the people that they could put their trust in Haile Selassie, and that whether things went well or ill he would see that their rights were protected and justice done.

19

Welcome Abroad!

RAS TAFARI MAKONNEN had made two trips abroad when he was Regent. The first was in 1923 when he paid a visit to Aden. This was the first time he had ever left his native soil; and while staying there as the guest of the Governor, and rather to the agitation of his staff, he made his first flight in an aeroplane. It was not many years before several planes of various makes were acquired by him and a small school of aviation started.

In 1924 his wife, Waizero Menan, visited Jerusalem to worship in the Ethiopian church on the roof of the Church of the Holy Sepulchre. On her way back she passed through Cairo, and for the first time had some impact with the life of a great city.

In 1925 he made his first trip to Europe. Gathering round him some of the chief men of his realm, Ras Seyum of Tigre, Ras Hailu of Gojjam, Dejazmach Mulugeta, and others, he visited Egypt, France, Italy, Belgium, Luxembourg, Switzerland, Sweden, Great Britain, and Greece. From his journeys he acquired first-hand knowledge of western administration, of factories, hospitals, and schools; in short of all the means whereby he might increase the wealth and wellbeing of his nation, and equip it to take its place in the progress of civilization. It was during this time that he began to make those personal contacts and friendships which throughout his life he has so greatly valued.

Such a kaleidoscope of new sights and scenes within the space of a few weeks might well have bemused his party. A story is told of the treasurer who accompanied their trip. Some purchases had been made and the friend who had negotiated them was bidden to go to the treasurer, who was in Paris, for payment. He presented his bill and was answered with a puzzled look, and led up to the hotel bedroom. Pulling out a trunk from under the bed, the treasurer unlocked it with a despairing gesture. 'Take the money yourself,' he said. The trunk was overflowing with notes and coins from all the countries that had been visited, and the poor treasurer was bewildered and bemused as to the value and locality of them all.

The Emperor had special reasons for his visits and special ties with the countries that he visited on his two tours in 1954. He had also arrived, as it were, at a convenient halting place in the internal affairs of his own country. The house was in order, security was assured, progress was on the march in most departments of the State, commerce was thriving, the economic position healthy, federation with Eritrea achieved. He had the opportunity and welcomed it, to make new contacts and re-establish old ones, to gain fresh experience and absorb new ideas for future use.

His first visit was made in May to the United States of America. He has always felt warmly towards the Government of the U.S.A., who never gave diplomatic recognition to the Italian annexation of Ethiopia. He is also in friendship bound to them by the valuable financial assistance which they had given to his country in the past ten years, and knows them and their ways through the many groups of American experts and technical advisers who are to be found in almost every sphere of action in Ethiopia. His most valued friend and adviser before the outbreak of war in 1936 was Mr Everard Colson, who sacrificed himself for the Ethiopian cause, and literally worked himself to death. Now an American is governor of the State Bank of Ethiopia, another is chief engineer of the State Gold Mines. Others assist in the highway development programme, the educational system, in the Ministries of Commerce and Industry, Defence, Agriculture, Finance, and Foreign Affairs.

The following statement was issued by the Ethiopian Embassy in Washington on the arrival of the Emperor in the United States in 1954:

> The visit of His Imperial Majesty Haile Selassie I, Emperor of Ethiopia, to the United States is the consequence of his long-standing interest and admiration for America, and of the invitation originally extended during his meeting with President Roosevelt in 1944, and renewed by President Eisenhower earlier this year.
>
> The Emperor arrived in Washington on 26th May to be the White House guest of the President and Mrs Eisenhower. His Imperial Majesty's tour of the United States, Canada, and Mexico includes New York, Boston, Ottawa, Montreal, Quebec, Ann Arbor, Lansing, Chicago, St Paul, Spokane, Seattle, San Francisco, Los Angeles, Stillwater, Oklahoma, Mexico City, New Orleans, and Fort Benning. He sails from New York on 14th July.

This was a very comprehensive programme; it covered a distance of many thousands of miles and during its progress the Emperor gained some insight into the vastness of the resources of the New World, and of the methods used to exploit them in the most economic and scientific way. Perhaps in this respect the Grand Coulee Dam on the Columbia River, that had already irrigated 100,000 acres, the water running through 260 miles of canals, would be of special interest. The problem of Lake Tsana's water, first considered in 1906, is one that will certainly come to the fore within the next few years.

A speech made by His Imperial Majesty to a joint meeting of the two houses of Congress has made history. Present were the entire Diplomatic Corps, the President and his Cabinet, the judges of the Supreme Court, besides both the members of the United States Senate and the House of Representatives.

Later, when in New York, he paid an official visit to the headquarters of the United Nations. He was greeted by the Secretary-General, who said the Emperor 'stands in the perspective of the history of our time as a symbolic landmark, a prophetic figure on the path of man's struggle to achieve international peace through concerted international action' —an honourable recognition of the lonely figure who stood on the platform at Geneva in June 1936.

He made a particular point of seeing American soldiers in hospital at San Francisco, who had fought alongside Ethiopian troops in Korea. He visited the Oklahoma Agricultural and Mechanical College at Stillwater, from which so many technicians and teachers have been supplied for service in the agricultural colleges in Jimma and Harar.

His way back took him also to visit President Tito of Yugoslavia, and to see something of the country and its problems. Many of its nationals are now working in Addis Ababa and in the last few years a Yugoslav Legation has been established there. Thence he went to Greece to renew an old friendship. The Greek community is long established in Ethiopia and very numerous. They live not only in Addis Ababa, but in many outlying districts of the empire, and their contribution to the growth of internal trade has been of long duration and widespread.

The Emperor returned to Ethiopia early in August to attend to urgent affairs. After a stay of two months only he left again for a tour of Europe.

This time his journey was made by air and sea. He visited many places already known to him, and enhanced by memory. Travelling by way of Wadi Halfa (had he not

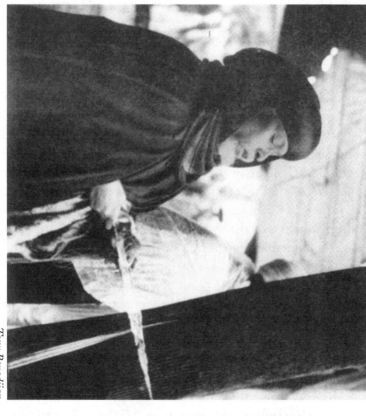

Archbishop Basileos gives his blessing

Tony Boyadjian

A group of children are at Dire Dawa (Harar province)

Lovelace

first set foot there on that return journey whose hopes in spite of opening discouragement had been so wonderfully fulfilled?) and Cairo, the Emperor flew on to Malta, where he was received with royal ceremony by the Governor and the British Fleet and met again a personal friend in Lord Louis Mountbatten, who had visited Addis Ababa in 1953. That is why a ship's bell, his gift, hangs in the General Wingate School. After a stay of two days in that historic island he embarked in the cruiser *Gambia* to make his journey to England by sea.

What memories must have been revived! What a contrast of circumstances to be pondered upon with acknowledgment to the Almighty whose strong arm 'shall break the nations in pieces like a potter's vessel.' 'He hath put down the mighty from their seat, and hath exalted the humble and meek.' Some such thoughts must have passed through his mind; perhaps he even chose this method of travel with special remembrance of the sympathy and comradeship on that previous journey through the Mediterranean in 1936.

Arriving in Portsmouth he was met with the same spontaneous and friendly welcome as had greeted him in adversity nearly twenty years previously. But what a difference as the train drew into the London terminus—not Waterloo this time, but Victoria. There might almost be a subtle intention in the change. Before the sport of fortune, the victim of aggression; now the friend and honoured guest of the sovereign. But the crowd that gathered along Victoria Street and up the Mall was the same—the man in the street who speaks for Britain whether in sympathy for distress or in acclamation for well-earned triumph.

'The station and neighbouring streets were crammed with many thousands anxious for a sight of the Emperor, and when he alighted he was wildly cheered.' That description, written about his arrival in 1936, would suit either occasion.

His visits in England were more personal and intimate affairs than his tour of America. In his speech at the banquet given by Her Majesty the Queen at Buckingham Palace he replied to the Queen's hope that she 'would like to think that in England he would always feel at home' with the generous response: 'The friendship of the Royal House and the British people alone sustained me and my people in our lonely struggles. Such friendship and loyalty have earned our imperishable gratitude and friendship.' It is perhaps not out of place to record here that His Imperial Majesty has just presented to the English church, erected this year in Addis Ababa, a memorial commemorating all those who fell in the campaign for the liberation of his country.

A less formal visit was paid to Her Majesty the Queen and His Royal Highness the Duke of Edinburgh at Windsor Castle, and here, as the royal children pedalled over on their tricycles to greet him in his car, he must have surely felt at home.

Visits to the Middlesex Hospital, to an infants' school in a new housing estate, to a teacher's training college: all these were indicative of interests to be studied in his own country.

He found time for a visit to his own house in Bath, where he was greeted with warm remembrance. He was given the freedom of the city, proud to welcome her royal citizen to his home again.

So the grand tour went on; to Paris next, for with the French people the Emperor has old associations. The railway line which for many years served as the link between Ethiopia and the outside world was a French project and has kept him in touch with that country.

His next visit was to Holland, and here again he stayed with the reigning Queen and her consort. During the last ten years relations with Holland have greatly expanded. Dutch advisers were among the Emperor's assistants in the task of

H.I.M. the Emperor, with H.M. Queen Elizabeth and the Duke of Edinburgh, driving through the gates of Buckingham Palace, October 1954

The Church of Selassie, and priests' ceremonial dance

reconstruction, and a very large Ethiopian-Dutch enterprise is entering its third year of existence. This is the Wonji Sugar Estate, which is one of the most important agricultural enterprises in the country. Covering an acreage of several thousand this extremely important and hopeful scheme plans to cut out the import of sugar within a very few years, and will be one of the most economically useful projects in the country. He visited a school for the blind, an enterprise with which he is very interested in Addis Ababa and at which he is a frequent visitor.

From Holland he crossed to Sweden, the country that has the oldest educational links with Ethiopia. It was on a previous visit that the Emperor said: 'Swedish missionaries have performed in my country a great and blessed work. They have founded schools and hospitals, they speak our language, and they of all missionaries have learnt how to win the affection and trust of my people.'

Through Norway he passed—there was an exhibition of Ethiopian art at Oslo, which he visited; then through Germany and up the Rhine to Switzerland. What a host of memories must have thronged him in that city to which he had come many years ago to plead his cause.

The hundreds of photographs which have illustrated the Emperor's travels are the best indication of his enjoyment of this 'part of experience,' as said the philosopher. Now he is home again 'to prick in some flowers of that he hath learned abroad into the customs of his own country.'

20

Silver Jubilee

THE years 1920—1930—1940—1955! Let us look at these milestones on the road to Silver Jubilee.

1920. Four years after the revolution which had put Ras Tafari at the head of the reform party, with Menelek's daughter on the throne, and the old Fitaurari holding the scales.

The only way to reach Addis Ababa was to come up by the train from Djibuti, spending three days on the journey, for it was not considered safe to travel by night. The Danakil tribes found the lengths of railway line convenient for melting down and beating into spearheads, and a night raid might remove a few hundred yards. About 4.30 the train would toil wearily into the station—nothing but a collection of tin-roofed huts along the line. There all the foreign population would be gathered—for there was not much other distraction in Addis Ababa of 1920—and the station was quite a pleasant afternoon ride through the fields and lanes, to rendezvous with old friends and meet new ones.

Three curious conveyances awaited us: an elegant victoria with a lace frilled hood, and a couple of traps for the luggage. We cantered up the steep mud slope that led to the centre of the town with a mounted retinue of friends and acquaintances alongside. We passed through the gates set where the road narrows at the top of modern Churchill Road, past the old post office and the few, very few, shops, out of the gates again that marked the eastern edge of the town, where the State Bank now stands, and away over the Makonnen bridge, with no protecting rail and half its present width. So out we went into the lanes and mud track that led across the Kabana—not by the English bridge, for that was a pile of odd masonry with a four-foot drop the other side—but a road wound round past the gates of the German Legation and over a narrow bridge that led up to the old Imperial Russian Legation that was to be our home.

The very next day on that narrow bridge we came face to face with the only car in Addis Ababa. It had been a gift from the Italians to the Empress Zauditu and was used perhaps once or twice a year. Both ponies reared and the back wheel went over the edge.

But it was pushed on again and we continued our journey to the open polo ground and racecourse—that wonderful spread of open meadow land, unfenced and open to all, which lay between the little ghibbi and the Kabana river. There was no new palace, for Ras Tafari lived, as did most people in those days, in a modest house of wattle and daub with a tin roof, and a long veranda where his visitors waited admittance.

A long narrow audience chamber, raised at one end, with fine rugs and a row of straight-backed chairs on either side, opened out of a small antechamber; their Highnesses sat on two gilt chairs facing down the room, and there were often a pair of young lion cubs playing about our ankles.

Every day the Regent rode down from his house to the big ghibbi which Menelek had built, where the Empress had her audience chamber in the little three-storeyed building that still stands over the main entrance. He would be accompanied by several hundred men-at-arms of his personal retinue—the bodyguard to be—the soldiers in their narrow white trousers and long shirts with the loin-cloth wound tight round and round their waists, and their rifles over their shoulders.

Just as in his early provincial days, anyone with a petition or a grievance might stand on the road with a stone or a pole on his shoulder and solicit attention; the Ras would nod to an attendant to find out the matter and bring it later to his notice. Sometimes a group would be sitting there uttering in unison the cry 'Abet! Abet!' and prostrating themselves as he passed. The appeal was always heard.

No cars, no conveyances of any kind apart from two or three dog-carts maintained by the legations, but seldom used, for we rode out to lunch, to tennis, to dinner with a hurricane lamp swinging—or once in Harar with torches carried flaming alongside us to dine with Ras Imeru, back again in Harar as Governor in 1924—to receptions at the ghibbi, often lasting from ten to four, to church service next to the Bololakos hotel. Immense courtesy everywhere— friendly faces, and shy but smiling children. A paperchase through the outskirts of the town once drew a horde of rushing helpers, eager, even to the extent of using their rifles, to help us catch the thieves. No police by day but a few night watchmen about the streets to call out 'Who's there?' and be content with the answer 'It is I.'

The presentation of credentials was a picturesque affair— a richly decked mule was provided by the Empress and sent with an army some thousand strong to the legation. Mounted on this in his uniform and plumed hat the Minister rode followed by his staff—in a variety of formal attire, even to frock coat and top hat—on their ponies. The procession rode impressively among the eucalyptus-trees that fringed the road.

Along the same road I saw the army pass the following year when the Regent, who had left the town a few days previously, brought in the prisoner Lij Yasu after his five years' wandering among the Danakil. They were a motley crowd, rejoicing as they came along, the chiefs in their finery, striped silk shirt, cloak, and lion's mane circlet.

1930. These are pictures of the past. Then the Regent became Emperor.

The old city gates were removed, the centre of the town cleared up and laid out, and here and there stone buildings began to rear their two or three storeys alongside the wattle and daub houses and tin huts, and open booths which had constituted the shops of Addis Ababa. It was impossible to buy even a safety pin in 1920; now there were dresses, *nouveautés* from Paris, knitting wool, even books and photographic materials.

Roads inside the capital were cleaned, widened, and metalled, so that by 1930 it was possible for anyone who had the fare to take a taxi from one end of the town to the other. The Emperor had his Rolls-Royce as well as another car— he once in kindness sent a small caterpillar pick-up so that my family might, over rough roads, reach his children's Christmas party in safety.

Public executions were abolished and the old tree of execution outside St George's Cathedral cut down and replaced by a fine statue of Menelek and a public garden. It was unveiled in the presence of the Duke of Gloucester, and the Marines' band from H.M.S. *Effingham* played the Ethiopian National Anthem.

Police had come under instruction, and it was a matter of frequent comment that, at the coronation, after only a few months of training, their behaviour and efficiency when the city was crowded to its utmost, with people, animals, and cars, were worthy of high commendation.

1940. War has been declared by Italy against the Allies.

There is rumour, tension, hope, and fear, where a population of 25,000 Italians are living in the town, and the new market area across the stream houses the local populace. The day of liberation is drawing near, though none are as yet aware.

1955. We have moved, not twenty-five or thirty years, but centuries. The modern traveller arrives by plane to an excellent airfield, with its waiting-rooms, refreshments, and well-managed customs barrier. The car that takes him to the town, about three miles away, passes along a tarmac road that has only recently been widened as it nears the foot of the town. There are five service stations for the 10,000 cars that now run on the city's roads. There are three large hotels and many smaller ones. Two of these have been set up in the last six years, more are projected.

Government buildings, mostly erected during the Italian occupation, of poor design and faulty construction, house the dozen ministries. Plans are on foot to move these eventually to the road that runs between the two palaces, which is now being widened, and of which the trees planted at the coronation in 1930 now make a pleasant avenue. In 1935 the new palace was built and furnished and this has now been enlarged and surrounded with a large garden and paddock, all on the original site of the little ghibbi. The trees planted between 1925 and 1935 are now well grown, and there is an ornamental pond in the middle of the central approach. The sovereign's car with its imperial flag and the escort of black uniformed motor-cyclists moves swiftly out under the decorated archway.

Everywhere there are rising stone houses of pleasant proportions, mainly of one storey only, neat enclosing walls, all the amenities of comfortable housing in water, light, and sanitation.

There are hundreds of school-children about the streets on their way to and from the twenty to thirty large schools that function in the city. There are ambulances for the hospitals. Perhaps one rather misses the courtesy and shyness of the old days. Much of this has been lost in the advent of modern education—in the rush to catch up with the outside world, which has come to them in the papers, in the cinema, in the impact of so many foreign advisers and helpers. It is a problem for the schools to face up to: the combination of a liberal teaching with an ordered discipline, to temper freedom with the spirit of service.

In the old days, when the Phelps Stokes Educational Commission asked the boys in the schools of 1924 'What made you wish to come to school?' the invariable reply was 'I wish to fit myself to serve my country.' Just this answer might the Emperor have given himself a few years earlier. But for the most part the young people of to-day have come too easily by their benefits and there is more talk of 'rights' than of 'privileges.' Here is where the Church must keep pace with the times. In most schools there is no religious training of the same liberal attitude as the teaching in other subjects, in some there is none at all. It is a matter for disquietude that the empty house, swept and garnished, may house devils that are worse than the old spirits of ignorance and poverty, dirt and disease. But of these problems the Emperor is well aware.

Up this year will go the triumphal arches, the pillars with their flags and decorations. Out will stream the populace, cleaner, better dressed, more alert to see and know all that is new and interesting and modern.

Over it all presides the genius of its ruler. He observes all, criticizes, designs, constructs. What manner of man he is these pages will have shown. May his people take an example from his supreme patience, steady perseverance, unquenchable ardour, and strong faith.   Above all comes the spirit that animates, for 'without vision the people perish.'

There will be rejoicing, feasting, and in the heart of the sovereign a profound gratitude.

'Thou, Almighty God, hast led me to finish what by Thy will Thou didst cause me to begin.'

21

The Man

LITTLE has been said in these pages about the private life of His Majesty the Emperor. Crowded though his day is, it would be wrong to think that his home and his family do not find their share of his time.

He has three sons and one surviving daughter, Princess Tenagne Worq, whose second husband is the Emperor's representative in Eritrea. Her family by her first husband, Ras Desta, were all educated in England. Her eldest daughter is already married and has three children. Her only surviving son is a midshipman on H.M.S. *Triumph*. The Emperor's two elder sons, the Crown Prince and the Duke of Harar, are both married, and the grandchildren and great-grandchildren are constant visitors at the palace; in fact one house in the grounds is always reserved for them. The succession is safeguarded in the eighteen months' old baby son of the Crown Prince. The Duke of Harar has also three young sons. It does not take long to find out that the Emperor is fond of children, and that children are natural and happy in his presence. I well remember that at a picnic in the forest given in honour of Lord Montgomery, after lunch the Emperor suggested a walk, waving his hand to the children. They immediately surged up and set off with him through the trees, laughing and chattering. His Christmas party is an eagerly expected event. When he visited the English school every child felt that he had somehow noticed each of them. Many photographs bear witness to this mutual enjoyment. I have seen him keep his own entourage waiting for a quarter of an hour, while he sat at a table talking to boys and girls at an educational exhibition. When he visits an exhibition or a sports event children are frequently standing at the back of his chair. Animals too, find a natural friend in him. His little dog accompanies him everywhere.

The first impression he gives is that of great natural dignity and charm of manner. You cannot mistake but that he is the Emperor descended from a long line of kings, and he himself never forgets it. At the same time he is charming and courteous as host, always giving you the feeling that you are welcome; or as guest putting you at your ease and interested and appreciative of what you have to show. With his sons he spent a day last year on a second visit to our farm The pleasure he gave was unalloyed.

Amongst his own people he moves freely and is very approachable. He drives, except on ceremonial occasions, without escort and, as has been said, drops in without warning in a friendly way on hospitals, schools, and other institutions in which he is interested.

You hear on all sides of little acts of kindness and thoughtfulness. An amateur photographer will tell you how she was trying to get a snapshot and was not expert enough to seize the opportunity, and how the Emperor, seeing her difficulty, stopped and posed for her. Schoolmasters will tell of presents of grapes sent to his boys from the Emperor's gardens. My husband recalls how during the campaign he arrived at the Emperor's camp long after midnight to make a report to the Emperor, and after he had done this he found the Emperor's spare bed prepared for him, and, on his leaving again at dawn an English breakfast set ready for him under a tree.

If your duties or opportunities bring you into closer contact with him, you find the Emperor easy to approach, receptive of new ideas and willing to listen to your point of view. You hear that, if he thinks they are doing their best, he is patient with his officials and helpful to them in their difficulties; but that he can be very severe in cases of what he believes to be wilful negligence. Once the Emperor has given his confidence to one of his ministers or assistants he is slow to withdraw it; and it is noticeable that changes in his staff are infrequent. They return this treatment by great personal devotion to him, and this is apparent in particular in the case of his foreign advisers.

Whether you have lived in Ethiopia for a long time or are merely a visitor, you soon become aware of the fact that in matters of importance the initiative is seldom, if ever, taken except by the Emperor, and that nothing is ever carried to a conclusion without the necessary push being given by him. It is true to say then that the changes that have been wrought in Ethiopia in the last twenty-five years are to a very large extent his work. Of course the circumstances of the times have compelled change—the Italian aggression and occupation and the consequent impact of world convulsions all breaking down Ethiopian isolation and letting in a flood of new experiences and new ideas—but events and the inrush of ideas had necessarily to be guided or moulded to form the ultimate pattern of change, and the brain and hands that did this were Haile Selassie's.

In twenty-five years the whole system of government has been changed from a feudal one to a constitutional centralized administration, based—if not yet fully realized—on democratic ideas; this central authority is obeyed and public security maintained as never before; the national church has gained its independence from outside control and its new leaders recognize the need for spiritual revival; education of the masses starting from zero is now well under way; health services are spreading; communications of all sorts are opening up the country; the national economy has developed on modern lines to an astonishing extent, and still more strangely is balanced and healthy. The list could be lengthened. All this spells revolution and each of the changes was fraught with its own dangers. But it has been a peaceful revolution; and its inspirer and leader was the ruler himself!

His record shows Haile Selassie to be a statesman of a high order, and a most astute negotiator. He is very tenacious of his own point of view and will never give way on what he feels is a matter of principle; but at the same time he will not let non-essentials stand in the way of agreement. He is quick at getting to the heart of a discussion, to separate the essentials from the non-essentials.

When in America last year he was asked to address the Foreign Policy Association. This speech shows so well the clarity of his thinking, and his attitude toward international problems, that it is quoted *in extenso*.

The Foreign Minister of a small but supremely courageous state on the eve of the outbreak of the First World War declared that one of the difficult tasks in the world was to be the Foreign Minister of a small country. Surely, this observation applies to-day no less than forty years ago. For a small state, foreign policy is the very basis of its existence since arms can never, by definition, suffice to that end. Every small state, in the final analysis, is given to make intellectual choices if it is to continue to exist.

Indeed, to-day, one is compelled to inquire whether there is a prospect for the continued existence of small states.

For our part, we do not share this feeling of pessimism, although conditions of the present hour make the struggle for existence an exceedingly difficult one. We feel it important that small states should be able to survive and make their contribution to the maintenance of world peace. We consider their role to be of importance in the following respects. Small states bear an element of tolerance and comprehension that would otherwise be lacking to a great extent in the world to-day. These countries, having need, as they do, of foreign assistance and co-operation, have become theatres where different nationalities learn to co-operate peaceably. This is clearly the case with Ethiopia. It is not surprising, therefore, that history confirms the conclusion that compromise settlements most often proceed from small states. This is the case of the work of the United Nations where, if you will examine the numerous issues considered by that organization, you will discover that the compromise formulas that have been carried into execution have been those proposed not by a large state or states, nor even by middle-sized states, but rather by the smaller members of the United Nations.

Finally, it is certain that the basic support of the principle of collective security comes, not from the larger states, but from the small states which have more to gain and more to lose by failure in its application. In this respect, it is significant that the smaller states associated in the United Nations efforts in Korea outnumbered the larger states.

If, then, it is important that small states continue to make their contribution for world peace, and if, on the other hand, the development of power politics would seem to threaten their very existence, how can this dilemma be faced?

In the past there have been two possible solutions to this problem. However, the course of present-day events has clearly demonstrated that they can no longer be retained to assure the safety and independence of small states. The system of alliances was, of course, one alternative that has been followed in the past. However, the First World War threatened this solution and the events immediately preceding the outbreak of the Second World War brought it the *coup-de-grâce*. In fact, as the distinguished President of Columbia University remarked some years ago, it is doubtful whether the emergence to-day of giant states permits the co-existence of any system of alliance or balance of power. In this connection, it is surely difficult to assert that even the North Atlantic group of states to-day constitutes an alliance as such.

The second alternative open to small states was one based upon the fact almost universally true that small states owe their existence to their strategic attractiveness. The natural consequence of this phenomenon was for the small states either to adopt a forthright and immutable policy of neutrality or, contrariwise, to adopt the policy of playing off one group against the other. Although for Ethiopia a policy of neutrality has long been attractive were it only for reasons of geographical isolation, her traditions exclude such a choice, and indeed, the conditions of the modern world would render for any small state such a policy difficult of execution. On the other hand, Ethiopia abhors a policy of playing off sides, and events of recent months have shown that where such a policy is being followed it is productive of no results. Even where results are to be obtained, it is extremely doubtful whether, with the outbreak of war, they could serve to assure the independence of any such state.

Such are the problems with which a small country, such as Ethiopia, is faced. For Ethiopia there can be but one answer. We are convinced that consideration of political and military factors, advantages, and dangers to-day inevitably lead to frustration and impasse. No small country can hope to effect a decision which, in the end, will serve to assure its independence, when that decision is based on a balancing out of factors, for to-day no such balancing out can any longer be achieved. We can only make our choice and, to adopt an American phrase, 'stand up and be counted.' We must, in final analysis, make our decision on the basis of what we conceive to be a decision in the light of conscience, and of right principle on the theory, perhaps a mistaken one, that in final analysis that must inevitably be the decision taken by the majority of right-minded states. The events of the past twenty years have abundantly supported this theory which we have defended in the name of and on behalf of Ethiopia. The sacrifices of the Ethiopian patriots and of millions of like-minded heroes throughout the world have brilliantly proved that justice may be delayed but not denied. In reaching a decision in the light of conscience and of right principle, the United Nations itself is at hand to support us. It is gratifying to us that Ethiopia was not the only small state to participate in the United Nations efforts in Korea.

We feel that such is, in the final analysis and basically, the policy of the United States itself, and whatever be the difficulties of the hour, and however difficult it may be at the moment to evolve a satisfactory and precise solution for any precise event, that we will, always, in the end, find at our side the great and powerful United States, marching on the side of justice and peace.

Patience, perseverance, and steadfastness are the keynotes of his character—and they have stood him in good stead. But they alone would not have been enough to see him through. They are backed up by a deep faith in the power and goodness of God. Through all the ups and downs of his life this faith has not faltered and it is coupled to a great thankfulness for God's mercies to him. This impression on those few who saw him slip away from the pomp and ceremony of his reception on the top of the Entotto mountain on the day of his return, and were privileged to enter with him the Church of Mariam overlooking the city and see him prostrate himself before the Sanctuary, in passionate adoration and thankfulness, is indelible. 'The Lion of Judah hath prevailed.'

Postscript

MAY 19th, 1955.   We have been summoned to an audience
with His Imperial Majesty.   The gates of the private entrance
to the palace are opened by sentries in the uniform of the
Imperial Guard.   We drive up an avenue of mimosa-trees,
past the private chapel of St Mark and the house where the
royal grandchildren often stay, and swing round into the open
forecourt of the palace.   The sun is shining on the round
pond and the spiral of stone steps that run up to the flagstaff,
the gardens slope down to the main gates about a quarter of
a mile away.   It is here that the school-children gather in
their thousands to greet Their Imperial Majesties on special
occasions and on anniversaries such as 5th May, which we
commemorated this year as always with general rejoicing, a
banquet at the Menelek Palace, and magnificent fireworks,
and as always a new project to be launched.   This year saw
the opening by His Imperial Majesty of the new Y.M.C.A.
building—a great need fulfilled for the youth of the country,
and free of debt owing to a munificent gift from the
Emperor.

There is a red carpet up the steps that lead into the
entrance hall where a white-uniformed servant takes us in.
The hall has its long polished table with the visitors' book in
gold and crimson leather.   The Private Secretary, lately
promoted Tsafi Taezaz (Minister of the Pen), comes in a few
minutes after us, and the aide-de-camp arrives to summon us
to the audience.

At the end of the long corridor we can see the doors open
to the private drawing-room where His Imperial Majesty is
seated on the sofa.   As we enter his two little dogs bound

A family group

in and race across to jump up on the sofa by their royal master, and make themselves comfortable alongside him.

I had asked His Imperial Majesty if, at the outset of this Silver Jubilee year, he would add to the story of his life and reign some indication of his hopes and plans for the future of Ethiopia, and this he graciously consented to do, speaking with great frankness.

His Imperial Majesty stated that his first sentiments at the present time are ones of great thankfulness to Almighty God who has brought his people and himself safely through times of great trial and danger, and has vouchsafed them so much progress in the last twenty-five years in spite of all difficulties.

His next sentiment is one of hope and confidence in the future. There is much to be done; but with the courage, perseverance, and fervour for progress that exist among his people to-day much should be achieved, with God's continuing blessing.

It is with the idea of enabling his people themselves to take a greater share in shaping the future, and to secure their fuller support in the fulfilment of his Government's plans, that he expects, on the occasion of his Silver Jubilee, to promulgate an amended Constitution to perfect the present one. It will be remembered by all that when, of his own free will, in the year of his coronation, he granted to his people the present Constitution, there were many difficulties to contend with in its execution. The people themselves were called upon to achieve considerable political advances at one stroke, and this applied with the same force to other reforms. The final abolition of slavery, for instance, met with difficulty, and was completed only by his own personal intervention. In the matter of the Constitution, he discussed all that he wished to do with the 'balabats' (hereditary chiefs and landowners), and could proceed only so far as he could carry them with him. The amended Constitution, which will provide for doubling the number of the members of Parliament and ensuring that the Lower House is chosen by direct election, aims at giving the wishes of the people greater influence in the development of the country.

In the economic development of Ethiopia, his Government, as treasurers of the nation's wealth, have the twofold responsibility, on the one hand of seeing that money is not wasted, and on the other of ensuring that funds are forthcoming for necessary development. To achieve these ends they have worked hard, and on the whole successfully. It has always been his policy to make the basis of all development the advancement of education and public health. What has been achieved so far has, to a large extent, affected the larger towns only. It is now planned to spread education throughout the whole of Ethiopia, so that every person may learn to read the Amharic language and will have the opportunity of studying other languages as well.

The realization of these plans, and indeed of all reforms, can be attained only by the improvement of communications; and plans have been completed for the extension in the near future of the roads and railways. By the federation of Eritrea with Ethiopia access to the sea has been secured, and the Government are studying intensively how to improve the ports and their communications with Addis Ababa and other centres; financial provision is being made for these projects.

Other plans for economic development include the construction of the Lake Tsana barrage and the Koka dam on the Hawash river for the purposes of irrigation and electric power. He has plans for enlarging and improving his aviation schools and extending the air services, and for the development of agriculture and livestock breeding, which are, after all, Ethiopia's main sources of wealth.

Turning to the question of foreign relations, it is obvious

that Ethiopia can no longer live in isolation, and must therefore make her full contribution to the settlement of international problems.   It was not for pleasure only that he made
his recent tour of America and Europe, but in order to study
affairs at first hand and to make Ethiopia's position clear to
others.

Although the world is still living in a period of unremitting
tension and crises, it seems to him that the future has greatly
brightened.   The Ethiopian Government's sympathies have
been throughout with the people who have tried to solve
disputes peacefully.   All his life he has believed that the
nations of the world, living and working together as a family
in international organizations, should settle their problems
and disputes on the basis of peaceful agreement and collective
security.   The recent settlement achieved in regard to
Eritrea was acceptable to him, and in it he attained most of
his desires for the welfare of the inhabitants of Eritrea.   In
the case of the arrangements made for Italian Somaliland, he
would very naturally have preferred some provisional solution other than that which has been adopted.   He has no
hesitation in saying that he believes that, when the trustee-
ship comes to an end, the best solution for the future will be
federation with Ethiopia on the lines of the Eritrean solution.
He firmly believes that this will be in the best interests of the
Somalis, and that it is the solution which they themselves
will prefer in the light of their history, geographical position,
and economic situation.   He is aware that much propaganda
and many artificial demands are being brought to bear in the
endeavour to create another point of view, but he does not
think that this will affect the final issue.

The recent changes in the Sudan have, of course, been of
the greatest concern to Ethiopia, and she cannot remain an
uninterested observer of what is going on.   He and his
people, being lovers of freedom and having so recently had to

fight for its preservation, would wish to support the Sudanese, whose support and hospitality during his struggle for liberation will never be forgotten, in their efforts to secure and maintain that complete freedom of choice which is theirs as of right.

Index